RIDING THE WHIRLWIND

'Twas then great Marlborough's mighty soul was proved, ...
Calm and serene he drives the furious blast, ...
Rides in the whirlwind, and directs the storm.

JOSEPH ADDISON, The Campaign, 1705

RIDING THE WHIRLWIND

Benton on Managing Turbulence

Peter Benton

Basil Blackwell

Copyright © Peter Benton 1990

First published 1990

Basil Blackwell Ltd
108 Cowley Road, Oxford, OX4 1JF, UK

Basil Blackwell, Inc.
3 Cambridge Center
Cambridge, Massachusetts 02142, USA

British Library Cataloguing in Publication Data

A CIP catalogue record for this book is available from
the British Library.

Library of Congress Cataloging in Publication Data
Benton, Peter.
Riding the whirlwind: Benton on managing turbulence /
Peter Benton.
p.   cm.
ISBN 0–631–17757–4
1. Organizational change.   2. Economic history – 1945–   I. Title.
HD58.8.B463   1990
658.4'06 – dc20   90–439 CIP

Typeset in 11½ on 13½ pt Bembo
by Butler & Tanner Ltd, Frome and London
Printed in Great Britain by
T.J. Press Ltd, Padstow, Cornwall

CONTENTS

Contents

ACKNOWLEDGEMENTS

My first obligation is to those scholarly booksellers who
have allowed me to browse so freely, and sometimes
to buy books. Pickering & Chatto, Maggs, Quaritch and John
Sperr have each guided me to a stock of ideas from the past
that has helped colour the lessons of present experience.
Librarians like Sharon Barker of the British Institute of Management and Sarah Dodgson of the Athenaeum have been
tireless; the British Library has delighted with copies to
compare, often fascinating in their provenance. I have cited
quotations in the chapter notes; translations are my own unless
credited to another.

Richard Burton and the Blackwell team have been generous
with their suggestions, and tactful. Hugh Parker, Roy Giles
and Ronald Lessem have each read an early draft, and gave
invaluable advice that I have tried to follow, though imperfectly. Lecture audiences in more than one country have rubbed
some of the rough edges off many of the thoughts floated in
this book. My thanks go to all of them.

Finally, my family has put up cheerfully with dull holidays
at home, pressed into reading trial texts, and responded with
views frankly expressed. My wife's encouragement brought
me through to the end.

The author and publisher wish to thank George Sassoon for
permission to use lines from the poem *Base Details* by Siegfried
Sassoon.

FOR RUTH

INTRODUCTION

TURBULENCE is the characteristic of our times. Many find that uncomfortable and cling to old certainties, unmindful of their fallacies. Others believe all is new, nothing holds true from regimes discredited by contempt. But, "plus ça change, plus c'est la même chose", wrote Alphonse Karr in 1849, as the ancien régime was finally swept away in the year of revolutions. This book reflects on our own revolution: that upheaval in every aspect of our working lives, born of the shock of new technology unfettered by constraints on trade; the irresistible diffusion of knowledge. We too find that old values re-emerge, including some that have been forgotten for years!

Paradoxically, as the diligent microchip offers to handle our routines, a new humanism is breaking through where it seemed most repressed. The Corporation, in all its forms, can no longer rely on its own prescriptive rules; when the name of the game is itself in play, it must turn to its people for fresh inspiration. When the formula of the State is barren, the factory or the paper-mill is depopulated, human beings turn their thoughts away from the mechanics that dominated their predecessors, towards the purpose – creating value as judged by others. The message is pregnant, rather than the medium; and the message is between people.

So what is new? Everything, and yet nothing. For two centuries, since Richard Arkwright switched on the industrial age, we have been dominated by the mechanical. In the past sixty years, the Great Crash, the Depression, dust-bowl despair and World War II have caused most societies to prefer order to initiative, stability to growth. Now those venerable influences have lost their force; untenable in a gale of change, a discontinuity of historic significance. The precepts that have formed our minds and our values are from an age that is passing; their certainties are likely to mislead, now circumstances are so radically different.

What are we to do, now that the received wisdom of two generations and more seems replete with fallacies? What works for the individual caught up in the net of a traditional organisation, as it tumbles about in the new forces? What measures loosen the agility and inspire the initiative that turbulent markets demand? What qualities make possible that unruffled mastery of tumult praised in Marlborough by Addison: "Calm and serene he drives the furious blast, . . . Rides in the whirlwind, and directs the storm."

Fortunately we do not have to work out our solutions from scratch. Others have been this way before. An earlier feudalism gave way to its renaissance. Adventurous personalities developed their own techniques for easing the shackles; some prospered, some triumphed – and some were crushed. Could Erasmus, Luther and the earlier Abelard say something of value to us? Is our predicament so different, or can we see in our own microcosms similar circumstances? And consider St Augustine, writing his Confessions as the Roman Empire fell under the rampaging Goths; might his reflections on forecasting in turbulence be useful to the engineer or economist of today? What of Augustus, settling Rome into good government after two generations of civil war? Does his dictum on fishing with a golden hook help us to manage risk more prudently – advice that Napoleon III could have followed with advantage; and several modern bankers, on both sides of the Atlantic!

Fortunately, too, for those who penetrate the publicity and side-step the apologists, our own world offers a rich variety of wisdom and folly. The folly may be less easy to find outside personal experience, as the hagiographers canonise fallible leaders, but be highly instructive for the connoisseur of fallacies. And, in a turbulent world, that is what every open mind should seek to be. For even the most trusted precept must fall under suspicion when the conditions for success change, and perhaps the criteria of victory. We may come to learn our limitations from our mistakes, but our inspirations have a richer source. This book draws on a wide range of experiences, to recount some tales of success in adjusting to new conditions. It draws on themes that may echo earlier victories; themes still true, because they derive from human nature.

The scene opens with some thoughts on the structured world that grew out of the Second World War, and on the nature of the revolution we now experience. In a backward glance, it seems that the individual struggling against the constraints of feudal power 500 years ago may illuminate the options of men and women locked in today's procedures. Next, turbulence is the theme: reviewing some extraordinary transformations in manufacture, in commerce, and in the public services; collapsed trade barriers, and the new global Rialto. So what are the new rules of the game? When the past is no safe guide for the future, what guiding light replaces the analyst's forecasts? Part III suggests some new inspirations for a world in which the old certainties may only mislead.

In Part IV, the implications for the individual are explored, and new leadership styles. Are control and creativity mutually exclusive? Must enterprise imply risk; is catastrophe the uncertain nemesis of the bold? Perhaps irresponsibility is the nursery of disaster; obligation and authority are best devolved together. Who will prosper, and what can one do to survive?

This is a hopeful book. The service economy creates real wealth, and the fruits are for all. The conditions for a prosperous and civilised society lie in the proper understanding of mankind – the humane studies, relegated to the periphery in the industrial age and by Organisation Man, as pastimes for an idle hour. Technology and the hard realities of the market place are part of the human condition, not opposed to it. In Europe, the United States and Japan; in the advanced economies and in the developing world, those who work with the grain of human desire and prejudice know how to prosper. First one must understand; understand and be understood, that is the mantra.

PART I

FEUDALISM AND RENAISSANCE

WE emerge from a new feudalism, with a renaissance in prospect as turbulent and potentially as fruitful as that explosion of the human spirit 500 years ago.

The structured post-war world, with its cartels and protective agreements, grew out of a horror of disorder similar to the sentiments that shaped medieval society. Then too, some persons and particular communities struggled to express their individual capabilities. How closely did they resemble the mould breakers of today? What can the free spirit emerging from the conventions of Organisation Man learn from those earlier pathfinders?

PART II

FEUDALISM AND RENAISSANCE

I

HISTORY REVISITED

✤

How did we get here?

THAT we live in turbulent times has been noted by more than one commentator on affairs and their management. Some call it chaos. This book takes a less anarchic view and seeks to understand the forces at work, and to establish some principles by which the individual may prosper; principles derived from the past, and from observing and taking part in some of the more agitated developments of our age.

This is, encouragingly, not the first time that people used to a stable and predictable world have found the old certainties a poor guide to the future. Saint Augustine saw the Roman Empire ravaged by Goths; could he have come to some useful conclusions on how the individual might prosper when the known certainties are blown away?[1] Erasmus and Luther both deplored the rigidities and self regarding processes of late feudalism in Europe; but they used very different tactics in bringing change. Which was most immediately effective, and were the results entirely desirable? Are there some thoughts from that titanic struggle that might be useful to the individual today seeking some freedom, or a lot, in a great corporation or a government department? And what of the people who may enjoy the fruits of the new opportunities? Is the campaign for vocational education as valid, when the nature of work is changing so remarkably? As Lord Melbourne said of that slashing historian, "I wish I was as cocksure of anything as Tom Macaulay is of everything." Perhaps we can learn how to live with that uncertainty more easily, with agility and resilience – and with sympathy for the world around us.

First though, let us understand how we in the developed world have arrived at our predicament – and predicament it is to find ourselves locked in an apparatus for handling affairs that was designed for quite different conditions. Not for the first time, human beings have to find ways of remoulding society for new circumstances; others have passed this way before, and we have there for the reading another feudalism, and people remarkably similar in their hopes, who found ways of breaking out – and of living with the excesses of uncontrolled enthusiasm.

ORGANISATION MAN

J. K. Galbraith, in his penetrating book *The Affluent Society*,[2] described the forces on the individual: "our liberties are now menaced by the conformity exacted by the large corporation and its impulse to create the Organisation Man." In the 1950s, most people worked in structured hierarchies, assigned to particular tasks, governed by the disciplines of the Corporation and the orders of top managers who reserved to themselves the strategic decisions, and those that balanced the competing requirements of the separate specialities. Those organisations resembled vast clockwork constructions, with a myriad of cogs turning on their spindles, mechanical, each oblivious of the machinery beyond its own sprockets.

The commanders of the great specialist divisions could operate as independent potentates, regulating their relationships with colleagues in memorandums of understanding, treaties, and the apparatus of foreign policy. They would send their foot soldiers into the battlefields of numerous committee rooms, charged with the responsibility for protecting functional interests.

That this description is neither far-fetched nor remote, I would quote only that huge organisation to which I was appointed in 1977. British Telecom's predecessor, Post Office Telecommunications, employing some 240,000 people, and generating revenues at that time of over £6 billion a year, was a monolith. As the Carter Committee recorded in 1976, the first layer of management below the chief executive was divided among functional specialists; so, significant issues involving more than one specialism could only be resolved by the chief executive himself, or by exhaustion. Committees were rife and decisions could take years, as the functional protagonists battled to preserve their sectional interests. Because no one was charged with getting the job done, each specialist felt a prime responsibility to his own baron; "the pursuit of fruitless perfection", was my phrase at the time. Once agreement had been reached, it was codified into law, and the affairs of each individual were then regulated by the sixteen edge feet of Telecommunication Instructions.

In that introverted world, in which the individual turned to the rulebook for guidance and instruction, telecommunications was not alone. That bureaucratic concern for procedure, and the tidy administration of a self-determined system, was widespread in the first forty years after the war, and still permeates most organisations to their detriment today.

THE SPECIALISTS

Gerard Fairtlough, who left a successful career with Shell to set up Celltech, a biotechnology venture, explains the phenomenon of the large bureaucracies another way.[3] After the Second World War, as the new technologies in the production of fuel, chemicals, power, motor cars and so on needed scale for economic success, there was a hunger for the scarce human skills that could make those huge operations work. The strong employer attracted the few people who had those necessary skills, and used them frugally; that is, they worked in jobs that were designed to make full use of their scarce resource.

Slotting specialists into functions from which they could not escape was prevalent in the public services too, confirming Fairtlough's theory, I think. In the British Army, for example, no signal officer has ever passed the rank of major general, and indeed that goes with the top specialist posts of Signal Officer in Chief, or Assistant Chief of the Defence Staff (Signals). A modern Field Marshal explains: "I want my engineers to do engineering"! Perhaps that husbanding of scarce scientific and engineering skills explains why so few of the leaders of British industry have them.

Intriguingly, the Royal Navy, which since Nelson's time has admired competence more generously, has promoted its specialists to the very highest ranks; Lord Mountbatten, with his patents for engineering inventions, was perhaps the most eminent.

Now, as Fairtlough points out, such skills are not so scarce, and if they are, the new phenomenon of networking makes those special talents available when they are needed. Those who wish to develop particular capabilities can do so, and use them more intensely and in a variety of circumstances. At the same time, every sort and size of organisation can reach outside to consultants or to service businesses for specialist help, and set their own talented people free to understand the broader issues. Similar needs, but better solutions.

The value of specialisation was recognised early in the Industrial Revolution, by Charles Dunoyer, for example, in *De la Liberté du Travail* written in 1845,[4] and by Herbert Spencer. But when W. H. Whyte in 1956[5] described specialisation within a speciality; when, as he put it, masters' degrees were offered in public relations, or in the training of airline stewardesses, the corporate hunger for narrow vocational skills must have been strong indeed. It still is, but need not imprison the organisation in the strait-jacket of the feudal structure – each to his allotted station – nor confine the individual to pursue the blinkered *métier* in which chance, or the personnel department, first placed him.

WHY THE BUREAUCRATS?

Indeed, it is a marvel that these rigidly structured, inward looking and bureaucratic organisations should have persisted so long. Insensitive to the outside world, fixed in procedures and slow to change, they certainly look out of date today. But then they arose at a very different time. After the chaos of the Second World War, there was a hunger throughout the world for order, and the protection afforded by well-intentioned, avuncular institutions. Just as after the ferocious disturbances following the collapse of the Roman Empire individuals sought the protection of powers capable of defence, so too our new feudal structure gained support, until it dominated in its turn.

Here is Geoffrey Crowther, a great editor of *The Economist*, writing in *Fortune* magazine in 1941:

The public has not liked the results of leaving the profit motive unchecked and uncontrolled. It has demanded a greater injection of Order into a system that was previously very largely one of Freedom. In so doing it has checked, controlled, licensed, investigated, and taxed the profit motive, with the result that the entrepreneurial opportunities for private individuals have been substantially reduced.

In that age, when order was so longingly desired, he had to go on to say, even writing in an American business magazine,

This should be the more easily done when the system of private enterprise runs in double harness with co-operative collectivism, each on its own side of the pole – when Freedom is teamed with Order. For the great urge to the restraint of trade is not greed so much as fear of insecurity. It is the desire to protect existing business, existing markets, existing employment that leads one industry after another to try to "stabilise" its own section of the economy.

With the formation of the United Nations, and the Bretton Woods agreement regulating the exchange rates of national currencies, with the protectionism and segmentation of markets into cartels, Organisation Man operated in a structured society; *orderly marketing* was the euphemism. Confidential discussions between chemical industry executives in private rooms of a well-known restaurant in London's Soho, or more explicit cartels, limited precisely the zones in which competition was good form. Financial institutions each had their permitted area of operation; jobbers, brokers, accepting houses, and so on. The price of cement was fixed by mutual agreement among producers, with prices to the consumer defined by circles centred on the manufacturing plant of one company or another. Sugar, ceramic tiles, gasoline, all were made available on conditions determined by the supplier, in agreement with his "competitors".

With the possibility of breaking out so circumscribed, it is perhaps not surprising that most organisations settled for the tidy incremental improvements so characteristic of our recent past. With markets so structured that agility and creative initiative were not particularly valuable or welcome, organisations could with impunity allow only a few at the top to make the significant decisions, and could benefit from steady polishing by each separate functional profession.

An earlier feudalism

It all compellingly recalls that earlier feudalism described by Jacob Burckhardt.[6] "Man was conscious of himself only as a member of a race, people, party, family or corporation – only through some general category." Like our own, the feudal society of the Middle Ages also defined each person's allotted role, with the Church offering the only practical ladder for the individual conscious of greater talents than his hereditary slot required. That feudalism too was largely successful in bringing order out of chaos, and protection to the individual from the marauding forces that broke down the civilisation of Rome. And that society suppressed the creative power of the individual – just like our own strait-jacket, now splitting at the seams everywhere.

While fealty to one's lord generally brought an uneasy protection from the most outrageous pillagers, commercial success went to those particular societies that were able to arrange some lifting of the feudal constraints. For 800 years, the guilds of the City of London defended the independence of master tradesmen "within the City and its liberties". The feudal powers that gripped all the rest of the nation knew that commercial prosperity depended upon the freedoms enjoyed within the City of London, and preserved them. In Germany, the seventy-seven free cities of the Hanseatic League[7] banded together in mutual support of commercial freedom, and in 1367 defeated the marauding Waldemar, King of Denmark, after their historic meeting in Cologne's Rathaus. There was no trouble after that in preserving their independence from lesser lords, or from the Emperor himself; their spirit no doubt inspires their descendants today in Gdansk and Riga.

In north Italy, such freedoms were widespread too. The commercial success of Florence, Lucca, Milan and Venice was made possible by the independence that citizens in those cities enjoyed from the obligations and constraints of the feudal society that surrounded them. With the papal power for centuries contending with the Holy Roman Emperor for control in Lombardy and Tuscany, cities that were able to play one against the other were able to negotiate extraordinary freedoms – and to enjoy the commercial prosperity that followed. As Sismondi puts it, in his *History of the Italian Republics*,[8] the guild system, with free master tradesmen organised into commercial associations, gave freedom wonderful powers of recovery.

The organisation of the city may therefore be compared to certain low forms of life. Decapitation did not mean death; there were always nerve-centres capable of directing vital action, of reco-ordinating vital functions, and of repairing mutilations. So long as the guilds remained, so long was there organised authority present, the possibility of reconstruction ... of development and of immense recuperative and potential power.

So freedom was wonderfully resilient, once the individual grew confident in his own capability, and in association with colleagues. A resilience apparent in our own times, as the ancient trading communities of Africa, the Indian Ocean and the China Seas redis-cover their latent commercial skills and venturing spirit.

Cities like Florence might be convulsed, as Guelph and Ghibelline contended for power in the interests of Pope and Emperor; but within the turbulence, the individual was free to act. Trade, prosperity, and that burgeoning of the human spirit known as the Renaissance, were the fruits. The government of Venice might have been described as an aristocratic tyranny, but the individual merchant had a wonderful freedom to pursue his destiny; a freedom to venture that was pursued for centuries. Among the characters of the commedia dell'arte, Venetians enjoyed Pantalone, the mer-chant venturer type that had made the city famous. In one version, shown in Figure 1, the right side of his mask is golden, with the arched eyebrow and the taut features of an outward looking entrepreneur. The left shows the dark and morose character of the careful man of money. Pantalone was a complex individual; a personality blending the two characteristics of successful com-merce – enterprise and prudence, verve and restraint.

Feudal Europe was not without its commercial successes too, but they came from more fragile springs. Spain, in its conquest of South

Figure 1 *Enterprise and Prudence*
Pantalone in the Venetian commedia dell'arte

America protected by papal decision, seized, but perhaps did not enjoy, the wealth of the Incas by virtue of that monopoly. Even while it lasted, that great commercial success of the feudal world seemed to bring little happiness, even to the rulers. A Philip forbidden by protocol to tend the fire in the Escorial does not seem to our eyes a particularly enviable figure. Perhaps today more than one chief executive of a great hierarchy feels that he too is an Organisation Man. It is a strong personality indeed who can break free of the apparatus — whether that is directed from the banks of the Hudson or from the Kremlin. Prisoners all, *apparatchiks* gripped by the pervasive bonds of bureaucracy.

MORE FUN AT THE TOP?

There must be many chief executives who would recognise in Francis Bacon's words[9] a forecast of their own imprisonment.

Men in *Great Place*, are thrice *Servants*: ... so as they have no Freedome; neither in their Persons; nor in their Actions; nor in their Times. It is a strange desire, to seek Power and to lose libertie; Or to seek Power over others, and to lose Power over a Man's selfe.

His essay goes on to say, "Certainly Great Persons, had need to borrow other Men's Opinions; to think themselves happy; For if they judge by their owne Feelings; they cannot finde it." The tyranny of the feudal organisation reaches right to the top, with danger sometimes added.

Some great men, lion-like in their net, burst out. Mao Tse Tung, ferocious at the creeping regrowth of Chinese bureaucracy, the Mandarin tradition reborn, unleashed the Red Guards on friends and enemies alike. Let a hundred flowers bloom, may well be a theme close to the hearts of western venture capitalists, but it certainly spelt anguish for millions as an old man fought to regain his youthful freedom, or perhaps a revolutionary's pleasure, in the anarchy of his Great Leap Forward.

We might recall the extraordinary personal career of Pope Pius II, Aeneas Silvius Piccolomini, poet and humanist in his youth. That fascinating man succeeded in the feudal system through a combination of great talent and personal charm. Secretary first to the anti-Pope, Felix V, then the Emperor Frederick III and Popes Nicholas V and Callixtus III – first of the infamous Borgias, he showed an ability to prosper that may well be helpful to today's corporate hopefuls. Arrived at the summit of feudal power, the poet felt the toils close around him, and struggled free. He spent months in a tumbledown house, as his *Commentaries*[10] tells us, full of rats as big as rabbits, which, running here and there, disturbed the night. Delightfully, he tells us of the green fields about Tivoli, where he "often rested by bubbling springs or under the shade of trees, working with the Cardinals on state matters or giving audience to the deputations, which followed him wherever he went". But poor Pius, for all his brilliance and his humanity, died a slave to his organisation, fruitlessly searching to form a new crusade against the Turks.

When feudalism was in its heyday, even the greatest individuals brought freedom only briefly. In the early thirteenth century, St Francis of Assisi set an example of personal simplicity and sympathy; within fifty years, the General Chapter of his Order in Padua commanded the provision of "many strong prisons".[11]

WIT AGAINST THE HIERARCHS

Because even the most awesome autocrat has latent the sensibility of a free being, wit has been the safest mode for the reformer, witness the court jester, or Russia's Holy Fools. Writing around AD 170, in the benign reign of the Antonine emperors, Aulus Gellius gave his son one example. When 500 years earlier Olympias, mother of Alexander the Great, received a letter that began "Alexander the king, son of Jove, to his mother Olympias, Hail!", she rebuked with wit: "Go easy, my dear; don't inform against me. Juno will certainly do me mighty harm if you confess my seduction in your letters!"

It may not always work: in twelfth-century France, that brilliant individual Peter Abelard delighted the students who flocked to join in the heady pleasures of liberal thought. While Abelard tried to protect himself from feudal penalty through paradox, advancing his attack on established ideas under the cover of the contrasting opinions of approved Fathers of the Church, St Bernard of Clairvaux, guardian of orthodoxy, brought him down in the end. But even though Abelard's technique, shown for example in his book *Sic et Non*,[12] did not save him from condemnation at Sens and Soissons, his method, "rather carping in its excessive clear-sightedness",[13] worked better for a less contentious man. Peter Lombard, whose *Sentences*[14] became the standard theological work for 400 years, went on to be Bishop of Paris. Particular passages were formally condemned over the centuries by one *apparatchik* enquiry or another, and fifteenth-century editions carried those findings in all the fury of their wording – but the book and its ideas survived, as did the author!

Later, the talented and well-connected Etienne Dolet was burnt in Paris, condemned by the Sorbonne for an excess of brilliance in contending with established teaching. Dolet got it wrong in two respects; he was brilliant without being conciliatory, and he chose to attack the establishment when it was most afraid. In 1546, the confidence of feudalism had been shattered by Luther's onslaught, and the Counter-Reformation was gathering ferocity.

Earlier, Erasmus of Rotterdam showed how bold a charming man could be and yet survive. His *Praise of Folly*[15] shows his technique in its most developed form. A sharp satire on the feudal establishment, the book was written while staying with Sir Thomas More in Chelsea, London. Published first in 1511 in Paris, Erasmus pointed the wit in the 1514 version; "the interpolations are so successfully satirical and aggressive", in Dr Screech's phrase.[16] The reaction was alarming, and fearing he had gone too far, Erasmus rushed to the safety of neutral Basle to see the two editions of 1515 through the press, adequately protected in a free city against the indignation of the traditional.

Since that book, in its final form, shows us how a very clever man could write a bitter revolutionary satire on a ferocious feudal establishment – and still survive – it may be of interest today to a corporate Hampden with similar aspirations; the table of contents is shown in Figure 2. Erasmus writes the book as a declamation by Folly herself: it starts, "Stulticia loquitur" – Folly speaks. So his first protection against criticism was that any erring phrase did not

IN HOC OPERE
CONTENTA.

LVDVS L. Annæi Senecæ,
De morte Claudij Cæsaris,
nuper in Germania repertus
cum Scholijs Beati Rhenani,

SYNESIVS Cyrenēsis de lau
dibus Caluitij, Ioāne Phrea
Britāno interprete, cū scho/
lijs Beati Rhenani.

ERASMI Roterodami Mo-
riæ Encomium, cum com-
mentarijs Gerhardi Listrij,
trium linguarum periti.

EPISTOLA apologetica
Erasmi Roterodami ad Mar
tinum Dorpiū theologum.

Figure 2 *Explosive disguised*
The Praise of folly: Erasmus: Table of Contents 1515 Edition

represent Erasmus' views, indeed only those of a foolish person. Next, in his title "Moriae Encomium", and in the dedication to Thomas More, both through pun and deliberate statement he places the work under the protection of Henry VIII's most favoured lawyer, and a future saint to boot. Lest there should be any mis-reading of either his Latin or his Greek, he ghosted explanatory passages by a certain Gerhard Lister, shown alongside the major text. Concerned that he might be accused of unseemly levity, the book first prints Seneca's playful celebration of the death of the Emperor Claudius, and then a work praising baldness, by a early Father of the Church. Having shown that both a serious Roman philosopher and an approved establishment figure could play the fool, he ends the work with an open letter to Martin Dorp, a protesting critic from the conservative university of Louvain. The technique worked; fifteen years later Erasmus was offered a cardinal's hat, while the *Praise of Folly* remained an inspiration for centuries to the individual seeking to break through the constraints of a feudal hierarchy.

In 1516, Erasmus showed another ploy for disturbing the defences of a feudal organisation with impunity. In that year, he published the first Greek Testament seen in the West since classical times, undermining at a stroke the unique authority of St Jerome's Latin version, the Vulgate. Prudently, he dedicated his new book to Pope Leo X,[17] and proudly published the 1519 edition with the papal approval printed as a frontispiece in a splendid engraved border.

Erasmus' technique may well give valuable hints to today's restive individual, struggling for the freedom to create his own visions. Indeed, in my own organisation, I believe Dr Alex Reid played a rather similar line in winning freedom for the Prestel team within the feudalism of Post Office Telecommunications, British Telecom's venerable predecessor. He persuaded me to nominate Prestel as an "executive", free to operate outside the usual bureaucratic rules, with his own staff-grading structure, and able to poach individuals for his team from the great corporate baronies. He confirmed that licence to roam by persuading me as chief executive to launch Prestel publicly at Wembley, to a fanfare of trumpets. After that, there was no turning back!

Is wit enough?

However, perhaps there is a further lesson to be learnt from Erasmus' charm, brilliance and revolutionary skill. All his delicate man-oeuvrings to change feudal society from within were swept away by Luther's head-on challenge and outright conflict with the estab-lishment.[18] Whether a century of religious war, and all Europe embittered by sectarian controversy, were a reasonable price to pay for reform, or even an effective destruction of feudalism, others must judge; I prefer the style of Erasmus.

Many today will recognise that in corporate affairs too, those who play for outright victory with heightened emotions can sweep away the efforts of those who wish to preserve the best of the past while setting the individual free. Some critics observe that in the privatisation of British Telecom, for example, freedom from government control seemed to imply to some managers a release from responsibility to serve the public. And, while it may be gen-erally accepted that Margaret Thatcher's governments have seen the most effective dismantling of feudal control in Britain since 1688, many regret that her revolution has swept away some past values as well. Rather more Luther than Erasmus, some might say.

A modern Tuscany?

In the United States, with its historic reliance on the balance of powers within the constitution, we can observe a situation not so different perhaps to the political environment in north Italy in the last 500 years of the Middle Ages. When foreign policy can be determined in the National Security Council, in the State Depart-ment, or in the White House itself, there is certainly the opportunity for the energetic individual to act in a way that would have impres-sed the Sforzas of Milan or the Medicis of Florence. Untidy perhaps, but plenty of room for individual initiative.

The process can be quite surprising to the outside observer; who would have thought in the days of Organisation Man that the structure for telecommunications in the United States would be determined by Judge Harold Greene, of the US Federal Court in

Washington DC? All the great constitutional powers contended for the right to determine that pattern; the Federal Communications Commission, the House of Representatives, the US Senate, and the Office of Telecommunications in the White House. But Judge Greene took the initiative, seized the AT & T case for his court, and became the sole determinant of policy for what is arguably the most important industry in the United States of America. Most observers consider that he has made a very good job of it.

Despite the evidence of *The Organisation Man*[19] and *The Affluent Society*,[20] Europeans have looked longingly at American freedoms, though sometimes through force of tradition rather than accurate observation! The large corporations of the United States were closer to the descriptions of Whyte and Galbraith than of Jean-Jacques Servan-Schreiber, idealised in his *Le Défi Américain*:[21] "Confiance souvent un peu naive, aux yeux d'Européens, mais que l'Amérique place à la fois dans la capacité d'autodétermination de ses hommes et dans l'aptitude de leur intelligence." Would that it were so, many an American corporate executive must have thought in 1967! Now, twenty years on, de Tocqueville's earlier observation in his *De la Démocratie en Amérique*,[22] seems a hopeful prospect: "cette maxime que l'individu est le meilleur juge de son intérêt particulier." Perhaps in the 1990s we shall all enjoy the trust in the individual that one observant Frenchman admired in the United States 150 years earlier – with confidence that the personal interests of soundly educated men and women will add up to the best interests of society as a whole.

TIMING

As Dolet and many other talented individuals have found, timing is of the essence in tackling powerful hierarchies with settled ways. If you are too idiosyncratic too soon, and unprotected by the conciliatory cloud of an Erasmus, you may finish up in the corporate penal settlement, or worse. One man who got it right was Sir John Harvey-Jones, rightly famous for changing that cumbersome chemical giant ICI into a surprisingly agile international business. By upbringing, early career and personal interests a member of the

British upper middle class, Harvey-Jones chose to mark a sharp distinction between himself and the traditional senior member of the ICI hierarchy. A former Royal Navy officer, specialist in submarines and in naval intelligence, he amazed at least one dispassionate observer by his personal appearance and the dramatic figure of his first actions as chief executive and chairman of that great, but traditional business. He chose an unusual persona; shaggy hair and mess-deck language were clear evidence that this chairman was different. The massive assault on the numbers and composition of ICI headquarters confirmed that the difference was not just cosmetic. Would that style have won him the chairmanship twenty years earlier? I doubt it; then the oligarchy chose Sir Paul Chambers, a distinguished civil servant and authority on the income tax of India.

So, perhaps, although Sir Karl Popper does not permit us to be historicists, we can get a hint or two from the great protagonists of the past on how the individual can prudently challenge the hierarchy, and put Organisation Man where he belongs – in the history books. "Learn from the Wisdom of the Ages" was the foundation for modern leadership offered at the 21st World Management Congress in New York's Waldorf Astoria in September 1989. For the individual seeking to understand how to enjoy turbulence, and survive, that may be the best advice of all.

NOTES

1 Augustine of Hippo, *Opuscula, Confessionum: Liber XI*, ed. Ascensius (Petit, Paris, 1513), p. 153.
2 J. K. Galbraith, *The Affluent Society* (Hamish Hamilton, London, 1958).
3 Gerard Fairtlough, 'Creative compartments', *London Business School Journal* (1986).
4 Charles Dunoyer, *De la Liberté du Travail* (Guillaumin, Paris, 1845).
5 W. H. Whyte, *The Organisation Man* (Cape, London, 1957).
6 Jacob Burckhardt, *The Civilization of the Renaissance in Italy*, tr. S. G. C. Middlemore (Phaedon, Vienna), p. 70.
7 Helen Zimmern, *The Hansa Towns* (Fisher Unwin, London, 1889), p. 61.
8 J. C. L. Sismondi, *History of the Italian Republics*, ed. W. Boulting (Routledge, London, n.d.), p. 159.
9 Francis Bacon, *The Essayes* (Haviland, London, 1629), p. 54.

10 Pius II, *Comentarii* (Rome, 1584), p. 252.

11 George Holmes, *Florence, Rome and the Origins of the Renaissance* (Clarendon Press, Oxford, 1986), p. 48.

12 Peter Abelard, *Sic et Non*, ed. Henke et Lindenkohl (Marburgi Cattorum, 1851).

13 H. O. Taylor, *The Mediaeval Mind* (Macmillan, New York, 1919), p. 17.

14 Petrus Lombardus, *Liber Sententarium* (Kesler, Basel, 1488).

15 Erasmus, *Moriae Encomium* (J. Froben, Basel, 1515).

16 M. A. Screech, *Erasmus: Ecstasy and the Praise of Folly* (Penguin, London, 1988).

17 Roland Bainton, *Erasmus of Christendom* (Collins Fontana, London, 1977), p. 183.

18 William Roscoe, *Leo the Tenth*, vol. IV (Cadell and Davies, London, 1806), pp. 64–75.

19 Whyte, *The Organisation Man*.

20 Galbraith, *The Affluent Society*.

21 Jean-Jacques Servan-Schreiber, *Le Défi Américain* (Denoël, Paris, 1967).

22 Alexis de Tocqueville, *De la Démocratie en Amérique* (Gosselin, Paris, 1835).

PART II

TURBULENCE

IRRESISTIBLE forces break the smooth linear flow of events. The power of technology and collapse of market barriers put every established relationship and prejudice to the test. There is nowhere to hide.

For those who seize the possibilities, competitive power surges. The new winners think and act strategically, leaping forward as they catch the breaking wave; the diligent plodder may never catch up.

Public service and private trade, advanced economy and rural village; all join in, given the vision. With open markets parochial havens protect no longer.

Though the world may be global, it is not homogeneous – and *vive la différence*! Citizens of the world need to be neighbours to each other.

2

REVOLUTION

LINEAR FLOW

1957 saw the publication of William Whyte's *The Organisation Man*,[1] and 1958 Kenneth Galbraith's *The Affluent Society*.[2] Those two books, in their cutting description of corporate life in our recent feudal period, recall the tranquil certainties of the large corporation in a structured economy. For the individual, once through the mandarin selection routines, the career seemed to stretch ahead, not fully visible perhaps, but no doubt in some linear extension from the present. A bit like punting leisurely along the stream in university days, noting that all living things align with the stream of events, save the odd water rat or coot striking its individual path. But we should have been warned; approaching the old mill-house, the linearity of the flowing waters becomes sharper; sharper until the laminar predictable flow turns into crashing turbulence over the weir's edge.

Still, hard to be aware thirty years ago that what looked so patterned could change so abruptly. It was a structured world, with its cartels and protected markets, constraining the initiatives of the individual, from a past that could be measured towards a future that flowed from it. With dramatic change so unlikely, most organisations, whether in the public service or trading for profit, felt sure that steady improvement on a broad front offered the best prospects for prosperity. With major change seeming unlikely, or at least sure to be damped by constraining forces, agility was not the first requirement. Organisations were designed so that each aspect of the corporate task could be separately improved by specialists honing some particular set of skills. Cogs turning on their spindles. All of life seemed to be like that, with the broad scope of Renaissance Man clearly out of date in a complex world where human progress depended on the dogged efforts of experts, each advancing on his own narrow front. As in Flanders in the First World War, a few at the head of affairs with their staffs decided on strategy, the rest performed their allotted tasks.

It was an age of comfortable certainties, where the past seemed so good a guide to the future that people who knew for sure had confidence in themselves, and convinced the others. The business schools turned out clever numerate analysts, loving numbers and skilled in the arts of induction. With newly arrived computers making calculations possible that were impractical to the slide-rule generation, Organisation Man revelled in excess like a Venetian glass-maker or a Victorian decorator. Regression analyses, lines of best fit, and forecasts with spurious probabilities, all convinced the corporate leaders that the future would be rather like the past, and that the great rigid hierarchies, with their myriads of diligent specialists, were the one sure way of seizing the fruits. Philosophers like Bertrand Russell might warn of the logical fallacies of induction, but for most, inferring the nature of the future by extrapolating from a measured past seemed mathematical, and therefore inevitable. Francis Bacon's inductive method was dominant.

Financiers in making their investments predicted with assurance the price of agricultural land – apparently unaware that in Britain that price had been bolstered by favourable treatment for estate duty, which was about to be repealed. The extraordinary growth in agricultural productivity, and the enforced decommissioning of land from food production under Common Market arrangements were unthought of. The price of antique silver, of town houses, of copper and cement all seemed predictable to a generation of analysts who thought it was enough to measure the obvious characteristics of the past, oblivious to the latent causalities that could turn that linear flow into turbulence. Trade cycles, *kondratiev* waves; even the inconsistencies were marshalled into convincing formulae.

TURBULENCE

Now, however nostalgically we may look back on those streamy days, when a captain might safely steer his boat by the wake – as the American phrase has it – we have reached the mill-house weir. The irresistible force of information technology, augmented by the necessary dismantling of trade barriers, has turned that predictable flow of events into a crashing turbulence. The new technology can transform the ability of any organisation to win; in open markets, the best competitor in the world can reach any customer. In the simple linear equations of the last thirty years, those were the two latent factors – competitive power and open markets – that have leapt into prominence, turning the smooth stream into a raging torrent. Those who can harness the new forces will surge forward into new prosperity; Organisation Man will perish. No part of our society is immune from the effects of this revolution. In Ronald Reagan's words, "there is nowhere to hide". In manufacturing industry, in the service sector, and in the public service, the past is no guide to the future; we must seek a new lodestar.

RUN TAILOR, RUN!

"Revolution, isn't that a bit strong?", some might say. Surely the traditional industries, the largest corporations, and the public services can watch others battling away in the stormy water. Can they? Consider the magnitude and pace of change. Take, for example, the transformation of a traditional family business, makers of popular clothing for nearly a century in a wooded valley near Londonderry in Ulster. Desmonds of Drumahoe have seized the new technology, and have become a formidable competitor. Selling primarily to the great British retail chain Marks and Spencer, the firm has used new technology in a quite fresh way. No longer content merely to automate traditional manual processes, so as to save money or to achieve a few days' improvement in collecting cash or controlling stock, the business has dramatically improved the value delivered to its direct customer, by enhancing the value that retailer can deliver in its turn to the ultimate purchaser in the high street.

First, take the relationship between designers and the retail buyer. Desmonds' designers work far away from base, in the fashion atmosphere of Carnaby Street, central London, but back in Drumahoe their designs are set up on terminals linked to the factory mainframe computer. At each terminal, with light pen and mouse, the garments are divided into their constituent parts, each set against a simulation of the cloth from which they will be cut. Lapels, pockets and panels are taken from the menu in the database, and laid out, with computed best fit for the various sizes, against the checks and stripes of the intended material. The design completed, estimating cost of material and fabrication is not guesswork, with margins for error to threaten competitiveness or profit, but accurate and immediate calculation. The quotation can be back with the buyer in twenty-four hours.

To produce the prototype – or the production template – the computer drives an automatic cutter, and the garment, stitched and finished to a size previously agreed with the retailer, can be back with the designer, and on a model before his buyer, within two days. With facsimile communication and powerful computing, a factory location in remote Londonderry is no longer a disadvantage; one aspect of the competitive equation has been transformed.

However, that strategic gain is not enough. While speed and flexibility in the service from designer to buyer puts Desmonds in a strong competitive position at the start of the process, the retailer cannot predict in detail how demand for colours, sizes and patterns will fluctuate within the range, in each of some 300 high street stores. For the retailer, there is massive economic value in offering a wide range of choice to the shopper while carrying minimal stocks. The garment maker who enhances that value gains competitive edge. With a flexible manufacturing system, the time taken to produce a dressing gown in a particular pattern can be cut from two weeks to just over a day. The saving in capital locked up in work in progress would have justified the investment on the most traditional criteria – proven savings related to measured expenditure. The largest benefit, though, comes through the added value as perceived by the customer – the economic value of flexibility. When that new agility in production was combined at Desmonds with a fully automated warehouse, the retailer's paradox – infinite choice for the shopper with negligible back-room stock – seemed achievable at last! The manufacturer's reward? Profit and secure growth.

In this particular traditional industry then, in a family business, in a rural environment, the new technology made possible in one technical generation an improvement in competitive power that would have taken decades of incremental progress by Organisation Man. The technology yielded its full fruit because its use was conceived strategically, implemented across traditional functions, and the benefits seized wherever they lay. Although the technology may have been applied principally in the factory and the warehouse, the rich rewards lay in the market place – in enhancing value as perceived by the customer.

BANKERS TOO

No aspect of our economy has seen as much change in recent years as the financial sector. Not only have the two Big Bangs, in New York and London, removed the cartels and segmentation of the markets, but the technology has changed radically the way deals are made, controlled, and recorded. Certainly in Britain the ability for businesses to move freely amongst the traditional tasks of stock jobbers, brokers, market makers and so on, has been a stimulus to change not always happy in its consequences. No one, however, seriously wishing to compete on the new commercial battlefield, can afford to ignore the opportunities opened by information technology.

I can recall visiting the dealing room of a major London bank in 1970, and questioning the director in charge as to how he was able to appraise the net effect of all the deals that were being made by each of those individuals, busy at their telephones. At that time, if a dealer accepted, say, a deposit of $1 million for six months – or sold Deutschmarks forward – the transaction was recorded on a paper slip, and passed to the back office so that the deal could be recorded and the net exposure of the bank assessed. With thirty or more dealers active at any time, with buyers and sellers appearing unpredictably in telephone calls to one or other of the traders, the issue of control was a very real one. Allow the dealers freedom, and you might be very active in the market place, but the risks could be great enough to destroy the bank itself. Indeed, when the market really loosened up, after the fixed peg was abandoned for floating exchange rates, the Bankhaus Herstatt was destroyed during a June night in 1974, while its momentarily unbalanced currency portfolio at the end of trading in Cologne, was exposed during subsequent activity across the Atlantic in New York.[3] Later that year, Westdeutsche Landesbank and the Union Bank of Switzerland also lost huge sums on foreign exchange, relying on sluggish controls in a turbulent market.

Well, my London bank had its answer: "Back to back", the director said. No dealer could lend money or accept a deposit unless he or she were able to find simultaneously an exactly matching transaction with an undoubted name. If you wish to lend $1 million for six months, you must find someone to deposit the same sum for the same period. Very prudent, but rather restrictive when deals are fleeting!

Now, any advanced international bank, like Citicorp for example, has changed all that. Each dealer enters his or her transaction as it is made, through a keyboard into the bank's mainframe computer. The director responsible can call up at any time a summary of exposure, in dollars or other currencies, at different interest rates and at different maturities. If the sum of all trades gives a balance incompatible with policy levels, the director himself can make an offsetting deal to correct the position. If trading ends in London with an unbalanced portfolio – as the unfortunate Herstatt experienced in 1974 – the correcting deal can be placed instantly in the New York market over the public network or the bank's international data circuits, and so on to Tokyo or Singapore.

In a traditional appraisal of the Citicorp system, benefits would be allowed in saving the cost of manpower required to calculate the bank's position and to complete the paperwork for transactions. But those savings in costs are tiny compared to the benefits in competitive power that the new controls allow. Dealers can be unleashed like lions to seize market share, with top management secure in the

knowledge that any temporary exposure to a major adverse movement in the market can be offset instantly. It is then a paradoxical
benefit of modern integrated systems that reliable real time controls,
while pervading an organisation, allow prudent delegation of
decisions which previously would have to be reserved to a few at
the level of central policy. So a pervasive system of controls can
unleash the creative power of individuals – provided the controls
are designed to monitor and to modify rather than dictate.

REACHING OUT

In the extrovert spirit of the New Age, some organisations have used
the new technology to reach outwards from their own operations,
linking with those of customers and colleagues. Some years ago,
Mullard, an arm of the great Dutch Phillips organisation, provided
some 200 of its customers with terminals and access to its own
mainframe computer. The customers were able to search for the
particular components they needed, and reserve them instantly,
whether they were in stock or scheduled for production. In offering
this service, Mullard was seeking not so much to reduce costs
through replacing paperwork with electronic processing, but to
create a new bond between supplier and customer. Once a customer's purchasing officers had built their own procedures around
the use of Mullard's logistic system, a larger share of business could
be expected to flow where it was easiest to place the orders. Should
a new competitor arrive on the scene, there would be strengthened
resistance to changing the supplier. A further example of information technology used strategically, to reinforce competitive
power.

In Britain, banks and building societies are following similar
principles in offering customers free terminals and access to the
bank's computers for financial transactions. Interestingly, first into
the field were the outsiders. A small home loan institution, the
Nottingham Building Society, saw the opportunity of expanding
beyond its local base in the Midlands. The Bank of Scotland, strong
north of the border but without partners in the rest of the country,
saw an opportunity to build a retail clientele without the traditional

expense of opening bank branches on expensive high street sites. Citicorp has creatively attached its own operations to those of a British government-inspired service for exporters. In offering the business customers of the Export Intelligence Service (EIS) an electronic facility for forward currency transactions, Citicorp has linked its financial services directly to business customers, at the time they are most likely to need them. Each day EIS takes a magnetic tape from the British Overseas Trade Board that lists business opportunities which have been identified by commercial sections of British embassies throughout the world.

The Ford Motor Company, encouraged perhaps by Toyota, is taking use of the technology another stage, by linking its own operations to those upstream and downstream in the value chain. After several years in the first stage of interconnection, with auto distributors able to co-operate with each other in locating particular models, using a central database managed by the car manufacturer, Ford has decided to go further. It is now possible, as the Japanese have shown, to have what some have referred to as "mass production of one", using computer controlled flexible manufacturing and assembly systems. If regular buyers of vehicles – fleet owners and the like – can be linked electronically through the regular distributors to the logistic system of the assembly plant; and if, moreover, that plant can be linked backwards to the suppliers of components and of sub-systems, it seems possible to create a sharp jump in value as perceived by the customer. Such a system offers the customer an exact permutation of features as fast as though he had ordered Henry Ford's famous black Model T of sixty years ago. By promoting a technology standard – as General Motors have done too – Ford can use its commercial power to insist that suppliers and distributors alike co-operate in creating an integral system. Then inefficient resources – idle work in progress and slowly moving variants – drop out, giving the measurable savings that please the accountants. The largest benefits though will surely lie in pleasing the customer, and the market share that will follow.

STRUCTURES FOR CHOICE

While the new technology, boldly used, can change the prospects for businesses in traditional industries, the most dramatic transformations can be won by those operating in the advanced technologies themselves. With electronic components showing for some twenty years now a progressive improvement in power of some 25 to 40 per cent each year, compound, the benefits of rapid development of new products can be dramatic. An extraordinary example is given by the improvement in cost effectiveness of the all-important central processor for the System X digital telephone exchanges. In one technical generation, the processor size was reduced from seven racks of equipment to one-half, and its power increased ten-fold. In less than two years, the System X consortium was capable of delivering a one hundred-fold improvement in processor power for every pound sterling of capital cost. Sadly, the deplorable effects of cost-plus pricing delayed that economic benefit for several years, seriously damaging the progress of System X in the international market place. Once again, a cartel-like arrangement from the feudal age thwarted the due harvest from technical brilliance.

The development of System X, although carried out in the most unpromising circumstances – with four independent partners, 2,500 design engineers working on eight separate sites – did show how the new technology could overcome, at least in part, the structural disadvantages of the project. In 1977, with rudimentary project control and hesitant use of computer aided design in the development process, it took more than sixty weeks to move from the engineering specification for a sub-system to a tested prototype, ready for manufacture. Once the strategic significance of speed had been grasped, each of the four parties – BT, GEC, STC and Plessey – combined in using the full capability of the technology to shorten that lead time dramatically.

Two-thirds of expended time was saved by building a consistent design system right from the first definition of function, through to the instructions for automatic machines to drill the printed circuit boards and insert the components. Logic design, simulation to confirm the desired functionality, spatial layout, masks for producing circuit designs on the printed circuit boards, and the tapes for controlling automatic drilling and inserting machines; all designed in a consecutive and harmonious sequence, with information flowing automatically in the computers, from one step to the next. The standards necessary to define how one piece of equipment related to another, and how one set of software instructions developed in Coventry would be sure to work smoothly with another element from Poole in Dorset or Martlesham in Suffolk, were indispensable – and were built into the system.

The benefits lay not so much in the reduction of cost as in the ability to use the power of new components quickly, and to respond flexibly to market needs. Others do it too: Seiko in Japan can design a new watch and start manufacture in three weeks; Honda can overwhelm a competitor with new products and Toyota bring a new motor car design to the factory floor in two years; everywhere, the bold and systematic use of computer aided design and manufacture slashes the time taken to introduce new products. That speeds the response to changing needs in a turbulent market place; that matches the very latest technology to the customer's latest need.

A Japanese house-builder offers his customers the chance to design their own homes directly through the computer. Permuting standard modules, the living-room can be longer, facing west instead of south, with more windows or fewer – all in response to the customer's desire; mass markets of one, designed for the individual, but with the economics of Henry Ford's Model T.

SERVING THE PUBLIC

While the power of the new technology is inescapable in the trading sector, now rapidly losing the barriers to competition, the opportunities in the public services can be irresistible too. So often introverted, the public service bureaucracies can seize the opportunities that matter to their clients only when they look outwards – towards the client. In this field also, merely mechanising traditional manual functions brings relatively meagre rewards. Creating added value in the eyes of the consumer generates the rich harvests.

In the West Midlands Fire Service, a computer system has been built that records the address of every premises in the territory, identifying the fire station closest to each in time, allowing for traffic and likely obstacles. Now, within ten seconds of the fire alert being received from the public, the alarm bell rings in the right place, and while on their way, the fire-fighters receive on their own mobile terminal a print-out, showing detailed maps, floor-plans, locations of hazardous materials and special instructions for dealing with them. Since damage from fire expands exponentially with time, the two and a half minutes saved getting the hoses into action has reduced fire loss by 20 per cent, showing a saving each year in property loss some five times greater than the capital cost of the system itself. The saving in life has proved greater still.

When a public service can turn its strategic thinking outwards, towards the beneficiaries, wealth can be created – or at least preserved – even though no money passes hands. The net benefit to the community can be far greater from one major initiative of this kind, than a decade of traditional incremental improvements in internal efficiency can ever have yielded in the past.

THE JAPANESE LEAP

Perhaps the most convincing demonstration of power in the strategic use of the new technology lies in the extraordinary progress that manufacturing industry in Japan has made towards the lights-out factory. Where so many European and American businesses have allowed the fullest use of technical opportunities to be hampered by the cramped calculation of incremental benefit, many Japanese firms have set their engineers the more stretching goal of completely eliminating the routine workforce in particular plants. The western calculation that the last handful of operators and tool setters does not represent a saving sufficient to justify the final tranche of technology, has proved to hold back the development of their automated factories by a technical generation. Once again, the commitment of top management, and those who provide the funds, to the full strategic leap forward, has proved to yield the day's march on a competitor that has been the ambition of generals throughout the ages.

A few years earlier, a similar Japanese insistence on total quality let loose the associated benefits to manufacturer and customer alike that have made Japanese industry so powerfully successful throughout the world. A quality goal that recognised just how much of a customer's wealth may be destroyed when products arrive late, or fail prematurely. A key to success found in sympathetic concern for what the customer really values. An economic factor ignored still by the introverted men of the cartel age! Japanese success came from that outward attitude, and the determination to leap rather than to shuffle forward.

Japanese industry has now seized resolutely on time as the new source of competitive advantage, as George Stalk has pointed out.[4] For every example in the United States or Britain of information technology used to collapse delay and accelerate aggression, Japan offers a dozen. Matsushita now takes two hours to make a washing machine, instead of 360; Honda took 80 per cent out of the time needed to make a motorcycle; Toyota taught a supplier how to make a component in one rather than in fifteen days!

Again, Stalk tells how imaginative use of new design techniques has cut two-thirds out of the product development process: Mitsubishi Electric improved its air-conditioner heat pump five times in as many years from 1980; a US competitor, with its five-year development process, finished up ten years behind, as the gap in each technical generation added to its competitor's lead. In motor cars, television sets, watches and moulds for plastic cases, Japan produces the new in half the time, or less, of the usual western competitor's initiative.

NOWHERE TO HIDE

There can surely be no doubt now that new forces of irresistible power have blown away the smooth predictable world in which Organisation Man could prosper. With the commercial advantage of a competitor possibly changed ten-fold in a few months, every trading organisation must go for the full opportunity, providing first for agility, coupled with a sensitive appreciation of the customer's true needs. To defer a possible technical advance is to court disaster; Gillette showed us that twenty years ago, when they shelved the stainless steel razor blade to defer disruption to production and sales plans – and gave Wilkinson their opening. Customers offered a new freedom of choice in the products they purchase will not tolerate for long any lesser improvement for old times' sake. Stimulated to high expectations in the market, they will become restive with unresponsive public and monopoly services too. The revolution affects everyone; there is nowhere to hide.

NOTES

1 W. H. Whyte, *The Organisation Man* (Cape, London, 1957).
2 J. K. Galbraith, *The Affluent Society* (Hamish Hamilton, London, 1958).
3 John Cooper, *The Management and Regulation of Banks* (Macmillan, London, 1984), p. 241.
4 George Stalk, 'Time – the next source of competitive advantage', *Harvard Business Review* (1988).

3

A WORLD WITHOUT FRONTIERS

OFF WITH THE BLINKERS!

IN the opportunity of our times, as turbulence in technology and in markets breaks down the old rigid hierarchies of the 1950s, new freedoms bring great benefits to those who can form new combinations. The art lies in cherishing the initiative and creative power of each person, while harnessing the efforts of all those individuals towards the achievement of corporate goals.

While people, ideas, and products roam the world unfettered, individual customers, wherever they may be, are coming to expect rather particular treatment. After decades in which many felt fortunate to have the necessities of life, choice and yet more choice encourages people to be choosy. Global markets certainly do not imply global products, let alone global services.

VIVE LA DIFFÉRENCE!

Nowhere is this distinction between the freedom to trade world-wide across boundaries, and the separate and particular characteristics of individuals and communities within such an open market, more clear than in Europe. In 1849, Prince Metternich wrote, "Italien ist ein geographischer Begriff", commenting acidly on Garibaldi's first failure to create a unified Italy. Today a wise marketeer recognises some truth still in that dismissive remark, although that nation is now certainly more than a "geographical concept"! He realises that while customers in Genoa and Naples may both speak Italian, their communities are quite different, and individuals may be influenced by quite distinct attitudes and values.

In the early 1970s, I asked an eminent Genovese why his colleagues in a local company found it so disagreeable to declare their true earnings to the fisc. "Ah", my friend said, "you must realise that we Genovese have been bankers for six centuries, and that necessarily in our relationships with fellow citizens, our financial probity is a by-word. But Rome, that's another matter; many of us look on them as our ancestors regarded Francois I of France, or a competing German emperor – an invasive power like the rest that have disturbed the government of our city state over the centuries." Perhaps throughout all Italy, with a lively sense of history so widespread, the generations have transmitted an inherited dislike, captured in Juvenal's satire, directed at the memory of the appalling Emperor Domitian.[1] He tells of the pressure on the fisherman who caught a huge turbot, to present it to the Emperor: "Whatever is outstanding or beautiful, wherever it swims, belongs to the Fisc; give it up, or perish!" Italians have seen enough rapacious tyrants in their history to have a lively distinction in their minds between fellow citizens and the rest!

Just as a global manager is not likely to make satisfactory progress in a proud Italian city until accepted as a fellow citizen, so in France he must learn to distinguish between the values of a Parisian and those of a countryman in the west, where the Vendée resisted fiercely the Revolution in the capital. These distinctions persist: portraits of the hero Charette abound in local chateaux, and the marquis snorts "fonctionnaire", as the definitive description of President Giscard d'Estaing. The Mayor of Nice is said to have turned his back on the 1789 bicentenary, since his city then belonged to the kingdom of Sardinia and the Revolution had nothing to with his compatriots. Bavaria is quite different to the Ruhr; Granada and Madrid have very different histories. In Britain, popular wisdom draws a boundary just north of Watford, dividing the real people to the north from the rich decadents near London! Chicago, Boston, Des Moines Iowa, and San Francisco all present quite different characteristics to the perceptive marketing man.

In the developing world, new nations have been formed, linking ancient cultures of quite different characteristics. During the Raj, no European civil servant in the Indian Empire would have behaved identically in Madras, Gujurat, Bengal, or Assam. They are no more similar today, though all participating in the new global market place. In Malaysia, the Chinese and Malay communities may live and work in the same cities, but are formed by separate cultures far too ancient and rich to be merged in a few decades, if ever. The westerner would do well to appreciate that the courtesy and charm of a distinguished Malay is linked to a venerable sense of honour as fierce as that of a French aristocrat of the eighteenth century. Not by chance is the Malay symbol throughout the China Seas that deadly and very beautiful dagger, the Kris; matt, black and sinuous, it can kill before the victim sees the threat!

NEW FLEXIBILITIES

So, the new markets may be global, but they are certainly not homogeneous. But global they will be, as barriers to trade fall, and as the world's telecommunication networks advance.

Diverse markets and yet homogeneous products, for the benefits in global sourcing, slender stocks and fast service; incompatible paradox? Not perhaps with well-conceived modular design. Hiross, for example, centred in New York, a new transnational of moderate size in the air conditioning business, shows what can be done in one field where custom products have been the norm hitherto. Short, standard, aluminium supports and standard, square tiles turn any floor into a ducting system more adaptable than a specially made convolution of tubes. Small, standard chillers, and personal fan units, each drawing air through a hole in the floor opened by removing a tile, give versatile solutions to fit a computer room in Penang or a traditional office block in London – and yet may be produced in New York State or Padua. Perhaps there is more variety to come, as the world responds differentially to disapproval of halogen hydrocarbons and their threat to the ozone layer; but the modular concept will help there too.

Modular design helps cope with differing standards, and with fast-moving technology. In System X, the telecom central switches for example, when the new processor was available, with its

100-fold economic improvement, it could be slid simply into a new exchange – or an old one – because the interfaces to other sub-systems and software had been previously defined, and remained unchanged. That architecture makes it possible to fit any special modules also, that may be needed for an unusual local signalling system or network management aid. Modular design can greatly simplify maintenance; in that same system, remote diagnosis can spot the failed unit in a complex installation and instruct a fitter to exchange it for another. And the diagnosis can be made from the other side of the globe!

In the actual manufacture of objects, the new technology makes possible greater variety with fewer people employed. At the most extreme, a lights-out factory producing the processors for computing equipment uses nobody to produce a product almost infinitely flexible. The product, depending upon the information software stored in its memory chips and disks, may be programmed for any of a thousand different uses. If the processor is connected to a telecommunication system, it can be interrogated remotely, and reprogrammed to carry out other tasks. Indeed, in an advanced information technology system, the intangibles – software, applications design, and the training of managers and users – can cost five times or more the price of the hardware itself. Some would say that the visible equipment – processor boards, cabinets, wiring, and so on – should best be looked upon just as a conduit for supplying the real products – the systems and the information, without which all those gadgets are inert in the creation of wealth.

TIME IS MONEY

In the service industries there is really little doubt that the product is based on information. In financial services, for example, as Walter Wriston has so eloquently pointed out, information has a value declining with age. Those who have recognised this important truth have made fortunes throughout history.

In the last two centuries of the Middle Ages, the Fugger family of Augsburg used their independence of the feudal world around them to build an extraordinary network of correspondents located in every city of Europe, and indeed ultimately in China and Peru.

That network was not there to report upon developments in philosophy or literature, but on the events that would determine price and demand in the global markets in which the firm operated. In 1815 the Rothschild family in London had a carrier pigeon service operating from just off the field at Waterloo. Knowing for sure who had won that battle hours before the rest of the market, enabled that family to add to its already substantial fortune. Our times are harsher; after Waterloo, while the Rothschilds grew richer, the ignorant survived. They would not be so fortunate today.

So we have to work in a global world for two irresistible reasons; market barriers are tumbling, and added value lies in information, capable of moving anywhere in the world at the speed of light. Managing events on that wide canvas, stimulating the creative power of the individual, focusing on the particular needs of each customer, is the challenge facing leaders at every level in the world today. Some traditional manufacturers have shown how much can be done across national frontiers in products that are intangible. General Motors used a small engineering firm in Essex, England, to design a new sports model to be made in Detroit. The computer aided design system in each location was linked by advanced telecom circuits, which made it possible for designer and production engineer to interrogate each other's database at will and simultaneously, across the Atlantic. Ford of Europe link design centres in Essex and Cologne, several assembly plants, a transmission plant in France, and some fifteen European marketing companies.

Texas Instruments offers their customers for custom-designed integrated circuits, terminals that can be connected to their advanced facility in Dallas. In this way, the huge investment in a plant capable of etching circuit lines less that one-millionth of a metre wide can be recovered from customers anywhere in the world – and still offer each customer a service that closely resembles what would have been available were the plant next door. In Phillips, software engineers in Malmesbury, west of London, can write programs for telephone exchanges made in Holland to be installed in Saudi Arabia. British Telecom, recognising the number of talented software people living in Ulster with no desire to leave the province, set up a software factory there in 1980; some fifty people contribute to systems run in hardware hundreds of miles away.

Let there be light!

That the flow of information across national frontiers is irresistible has certainly not escaped the attention of that great feudal power the Soviet Union. When Solidarity first burst upon the Polish scene, it was intriguing to find that the automatic telephone exchanges in Warsaw and Moscow crashed almost simultaneously. That proved the point; the only way to stop information flowing across a modern telecommunications network is to help the technology break down! So the new leaders of Russia are faced with an intriguing situation. To advance, their economy must draw upon the commercial fruits that information technology only makes possible with the use of communicating networks. Engineers, businessmen, economists, and indeed *apparatchiks*, need to draw on databases within Russia and, for advanced information, elsewhere in Europe, in America, and in Japan. Creation of those Russian databases, and freedom for many individuals to use them, is just not compatible with the operation of a closed society on feudal lines. The choice facing the leaders of Russia is stark; open up your society and join the rest of the world in enjoying the fruits of information technology, or fall behind relatively, at an ever increasing pace. That same choice faces the leaders of those few traditional organisations in the west, that long hopelessly for a continued enjoyment of their sheltered past.

Western taboos go too

While dismantling barriers to trade between countries has opened up global markets in the usual sense of the phrase, the new freedom to trade across traditional commercial frontiers within a nation has brought dramatic change also. The two Big Bangs, in New York and in London, set off revolutions in the financial services industry. In Britain, the freedom of well-established institutions to move into what looked like greener pastures proved irresistible to most and expensive to many. Beguiled with concepts like "financial supermarket" and "one-stop shopping for corporate treasurers", many managers found themselves in ferocious competition on unfamiliar terrain. With more optimistic contenders than the market had room for, it may be that the most clear sighted were those reluctant to stray from the knitting they knew! But for those left in the battle, life will never be the same again. Brought up in the old feudal structure to operate in a narrow field on terms regulated by authority, managers have had to learn how to fight and win in conditions as diverse and as competitive as those faced by the new global marketeer, as he turns the leaves of his atlas.

The honeypot of financial services has not just attracted its own bees. In the United States, the two largest providers of financial services to individual customers come from right outside the traditional industry. Sears Roebuck and General Motors were not seen as contenders with Citicorp for the business of Mr and Mrs America, but each earns more than that great bank from their retail financial services. How did they get there?

Sears Roebuck, established in the nineteenth century as a mail order business, supplying farmers' wives throughout the Midwest of America with practical clothing and equipment illustrated in their famous catalogues, moved into high street stores in the early years of this century. In trading for decades with millions of individual customers, they built up that most precious of all assets in the commercial world – a customer database with a history of trading patterns and personal behaviour with debt. Just as Citicorp brought together all its customer databases so as to see where more business could be done, and to check where exposure to loss had become unacceptable, so Sears Roebuck launched into the financial market with a similar strength. Moving by acquisition so as to bring in the necessary new skills, Sears built over ten years a financial empire grouped under Dean Witter Inc., and a chain of real-estate agents handling some 30 per cent of residential sales in the United States. Synergy, which used to be rather derided twenty years ago when venturing across a traditional industry barrier was taboo, has started to pay off. People who buy houses need money, and they need household goods. Sears can sell them the house, the goods, and the money.

In Britain, Littlewoods, starting from mail order like Sears, but with a huge potential customer database from their football pool gambling business, are moving similarly to offer financial services. Their catalogue, for example, carries pages selling insurance services alongside coloured illustrations of children's clothes and garden furniture. Hambros, an investment bank, and the Prudential, a great insurance business, have moved firmly into acquiring chains of real-estate agents, to create in Britain some of the synergy that is so attractive when viewed from across the Atlantic. Painful, perhaps, so early in the new experience, to struggle in a sluggish house market, but no doubt worth it in the end!

General Motors has recognised that, after signing a contract for a house, buying a car is the next largest commercial transaction for most people. The General Motors Finance Corporation with its tradable securities, has seized the opportunity of all those trans-actions – people buy cars more frequently than houses – to open their way into the honeypot.

The oil companies too, in their way, have recognised that at certain times individuals have a general propensity to buy. Gas station forecourts, for so long regarded as appropriate for gasoline, lubricants, boiled sweets and wash-leathers, may venture further as this thought matures.

In Japan, the urge to probe new fields has become a strategic fashion, as Professor Gen-Ichi Nakamura points out.[2] Expansion into new technology and international markets is near universal; many are moving firmly from niches to wider markets. Matsushita from home appliances to the broader field of industrial and consumer electronics, linking with General Electric and Golden Star of Korea. Takeda and others have moved from traditional chemicals into bio-technology and the pharmaceutical business; from traditional fibres into carbon-fibre, and the composite material pasture.

While these responses to the new freedoms may look rational and admirable, we should perhaps recall that similar fads have swept the strategic planning community before. While first steps usually follow the sound precepts of expanding from your strengths into fields where past achievements, in skills or customers, give an edge over other hopefuls, broaching unrelated markets can be perilous. Xerox showed that in their early moves in communications – the expensive X-TEN failure, for example. Many bold hands in the financial field burned their fingers, as they found themselves in unfamiliar and over-crowded markets. So why should the steel company Kawasaki, for example, in its fifteen-year vision to 2000, have fastened on semiconductors, tying up with SLI Logic? Somewhat reminiscent of the 1960s, when tobacco firms started their move into perfumes, retailing, and insurance; when utilities tried to skip like go-go stocks to edge up their price earnings ratios! Rather more sensible were Peoples Gas of Chicago, who put all their efforts into finding new supplies after the traditional fields in the lower forty-eight states lagged behind expanding demand. Peoples succeeded, and for years served their customers and shareholders well.

THE PURSUIT OF ADDED VALUE

Breaking through traditional frontiers can happen within an industry, where traditional wisdom has caused companies to confine themselves to particular tasks in what Michael Porter has so fruitfully named "the value chain".[3] In an advanced technology, the Digital Equipment Corporation has shown a bold and successful strategic thrust forward from its base in manufacturing technology towards the services it used to leave to others. While offering complete systems, it saw designing and building processor boards at the leading edge of the art as its particular *métier*. Digital seemed content for Original Equipment Manufacturers (OEMs) in many countries to add the disk drives, connections, cabinets, and so on that form what a customer would see as a computer. Those OEMs could then go on further to offer application software, help in system design, and sign lucrative maintenance contracts. In the early 1980s, Digital seemed to realise that while its company took the lion's share of technical risk, the bulk of profit and, more importantly, the predictable earnings, were left to others. It was, in a phrase, leaving piles of bucks on the table.

Since that awakening, Digital's movement down the value chain towards customer services has been aggressive and highly successful. To the aggrieved surprise of many OEMs, who were indeed customers themselves, Digital now generates more than half its profit growth each year from these new service businesses, seized in such a determined way.

NEW COMPETITORS

In this new global world, managers in enterprises of almost every kind find that the new commercial battles are fought with new competitors, on new and unfamiliar terrain. Whatever the home territory may have been, whether defined by a country, or by an industry sector, or by a particular set of activities, or indeed by all three, the future will be more complex and will change more rapidly. New competitors will arrive without warning from quite unexpected quarters. They will be armed with new skills, and may have longer relationships than you have with your own customers. Where you may seek to offer only a product or a service, they may see the whole picture better than you can, and produce complete solutions, not just problems half solved. In the global world, the introverted specialist from a traditional hierarchy will not know what has hit him.

NOTES

1 Juvenal, *Satira IV*, ed. Rupert and Koenig (Pickering edition, 1835), pp. 70–86.
2 Gen-Ichi Nakamura, 'Strategic management in major Japanese hightech companies', *Long Range Planning* (1986).
3 Michael Porter, *Competitive Advantage* (Free Press, New York, 1985).

PART III

NEW INSPIRATIONS

IN a turbulent world, the only certainty is change; introverts and tramliners run out of road. As in war, the new leaders foster agility, encouraging the individual to respond to the opportunity. New structures provide frameworks to cohere and to protect the corporate concerns. New technology resolves the paradox: free initiative and prudence.

What criteria work? What priorities and what relationships take Organisation Man safely into the jungle? If the creation of wealth is the universal good, can its pursuit betray true values? If public service switches to private profit, who suffers?

A new lodestar: value in the customer's terms – but who knows best?

4
JUNGLE WAR

PASSCHENDAELE OR PENANG?

THE turbulence of today's commercial battlefield, its sharp sur-
prises and split-second opportunities for victory, has its analogy
in the battlefields of war. Since so much of human talent has
been dedicated to that sad art, perhaps the thoughtful manager can
fruitfully reflect on some resemblances.

When in 1914 the huge armies of northern Europe were locked
in the four-year stalemate of Flanders, the environment resembled
somewhat the defined and slowly evolving markets of the early
1950s. There were great thrusts, the Germans towards Verdun, and
the atrocious ten-mile advance in the second battle of the Somme,
in which a million men died. Those thrusts, however, were signalled
long in advance. The munition trains would rumble for weeks,
bringing up the mountains of shells and the reinforcement battalions.
A break through two lines of trenches brought headlines in the
newspapers and medals for the generals.

So what did that modern Armageddon do for leadership? It made
it feudal. In Siegfried Sassoon's war poem,[1]

> If I were fierce, and bald, and short of breath,
> I'd live with scarlet Majors at the Base,
> And speed glum heroes up the line to death.

All significant military decisions were taken by a few senior generals,
living comfortably in chateaux miles behind the lines, with their
well-dressed, red-tabbed staff officers, planning the battle on large
maps, shifting a block here, tossing a marker into the basket after a
mauling more than usually devastating. The battlefield was to these

feudal courtiers an abstraction; a disembodied military exercise similar to the war-games that the German general staff had introduced fifty years earlier. On the battlefield itself, where horrors undreamt by the staff burnt the minds of a generation, brigadiers and colonels were as much in the grip of the machine as the most junior soldier. A brigade commander might perhaps be free to choose which battalion should lead the attack, when the trench parapet should be scaled, and the password for the day. The power to decide everything significant lay with Army headquarters, who even saw that the lion's share of military decorations went to their acolytes.

Such was the effect on the style of leadership, and the behaviour of individual professional soldiers, of the special and overpowering conditions of Flanders from 1914 to 1918. Yet in different circumstances, and at the same time, the military colleagues of those red-tabbed supreme commanders in Flanders behaved quite differently, stimulating individual initiative in a way that still seems attractive. In Arabia and Palestine,[2] Allenby, in a mobile war against a Turkish army that held down a huge territory with exiguous lines of communication, launched a guerrilla campaign. In T. E. Lawrence, he chose an extraordinary personality to lead it. That complex man, with his human sympathy and passionate adherence to the Arab cause, formed a bond with Sheikh Feisal that made victory possible, and created a legend. Lawrence himself, illegitimate, small and intellectual, would scarcely have commanded more than a platoon in a Flanders trench, to be blown away contending for a few yards of mud. On a fluid and turbulent battlefield, he became a master.

Guerrilla war

Perhaps the most fruitful example of a campaign won through the initiative of identifiable individuals of junior rank can be found in Malaya, in the defeat of the communist insurrection.[3] In just two years, from 1952 to 1954, Sir Gerald Templer created in that tormented country a style of leadership that destroyed a ruthless campaign by Chin Peng, leader of the Malayan Communist Party, and his colleagues, many of whom had been star soldiers in the British irregular campaign against the Japanese a few years earlier. Just how Templer in two years turned a desperate military and political situation into victory, may be best judged through the men and women who served with him.

We can draw three lessons, valuable to a leader embattled in the commercial world. First, morale. Templer, newly appointed with his extensive powers of general management, made it clear that no part of the system was outside his personal interest, and that individuals must achieve, rather than follow rules. He opened up the government and military machine for private citizens of Malaya to inspect and discuss with him; he showed that he cared about them. Second, he adopted a strategic plan, in which the social, the political, the economic, the police and military aspects of Malaya each had a complementary part to play. Military victory was not possible without the social and political progress needed to assure private individuals of their safety from communist reprisals. The political transformation in a country approaching independence was certainly not possible without the defeat of Chin Peng's military forces. Third, Templer let loose the initiative and creative power of the individual: the brilliant Irene Lee, the young Chinese detective inspector, who tracked the communist communication system; the rumbustious Evan Davies, who hunted down Goh Peng Tung in his jungle hideout; the thirty-seven men of the SAS who got R. A. H. Hoi and his force, after three months tracking in the jungle.

That style of top leadership not only made individual initiative possible, it encouraged remarkable people to join the team. Evan Davies, twenty years later seen stalking amongst the girls of the Casino de Paris, for all the world like Edward VII, could never have been an *apparatchik*!

So a turbulent field not only makes a new style of leadership necessary, it makes it possible. Strong personalities, unimpaired by years of conformity to custom, have always been able to seize the new freedoms, and exploit them. The necessary skill in today's world is to create an environment in which many thousands are induced to open up their creative powers, when the grip of the Organisation may seem to offer a more comfortable and less disturbing alternative – as a thoughtful member of a Ministry said to me in Prague, a few days after President Havel's first election.

OUT OF THE CHRYSALIS

Ten years ago, Post Office Telecommunications was an organisation rather like that; many thousands of people capable of being individuals, but acting like *apparatchiks*. One or two irrepressible personalities survived, oblivious to their leery conventional colleagues. Some were so rooted by inclination and custom in the comfortable pleasures of administration, that opening a window just drove them further inside. For the majority, however, the nature of the organisation's climate determined the characteristics of their own response. The issue for a revolutionary leader is how to change the climate for all, when only a few wish for that change spontaneously. Templer achieved the change and the victory in two years; in BT it took rather longer, and indeed is still not complete.

In my experience, a new chief executive faced with the need to transform an organisation has more effective levers available than is commonly recognised. Although it may take many months, if not years, to change the direction of a great administrative machine if one works through successive layers of authority, more direct methods can yield faster results. Very senior *apparatchiks*, safely ensconced in their traditional baronies, are hard to move. When power has been agglomerated over countless committee room engagements, minor changes will be bitterly resisted. In BT, the first step lay in reforming radically the scope and responsibilities of the first level of top management below the chief executive's office. By taking an orthogonal approach in 1979, dividing the top responsibilities by task and by business rather than by function, two benefits flowed: the past demarcation fortresses were swept away, and the attention of the organisation's most senior officers was focused on the achievement of results, rather than the protection of functional interests. On a grander scale, that approach worked wonders forty years earlier in the Pacific campaign, when MacArthur and Halsey each formed multi-service commands. Surely the close co-operation between land, sea and air forces at Guadalcanal owed much to that cohesive concern for victory, modifying inter-service pride.

One military approach works less well in civilian situations. Templer brought in new men to key positions, and that infused new energy without sowing undue discord, because those who arrived came from other formations in the same imperial service as the old hands who remained. When AT & T imported several hundred executives from IBM and elsewhere in the 1970s, there was substantial tissue rejection of the transplants. Archie McGill was one outstanding marketing man who found the atmosphere too oppressive and left. At BT I brought in only a handful, and gained perhaps more solid change throughout, because the future was seen to belong to any who could match the new mood, and the new team was seamless.

FEAR

If getting the responsibilities right is crucial, it is also necessary to develop quite rapidly a more resilient and creative attitude to change. In BT, in 1978, new technology was seen, by many tens of thousands of staff, as a potential threat with unimaginable consequences. In an industry which had for almost 100 years been dominated by the slow-moving electromechanical technology of Strowger, and copper wires or line of sight radio transmissions, the news leaking out from the laboratory was alarming. Electronic telephone exchanges with no moving parts promised to disturb the steady linear progress of 30,000 maintenance engineers. Slender glass fibres capable of carrying 2,000 telephone conversations at once alarmed the army of transmission technicians. The fear arose from two causes: concern that a way of life that had been eminently predictable for generations was entering turbulence, and an inability to imagine that the new technologies could create opportunities as well as threats. The fear was real, and showed itself – as with the Luddites in the first Industrial Revolution – in resistance to change, and a belief that retreat behind the walls of monopoly privilege was the safest course of action. Faced with such attitudes pervasive throughout an organisation, any chief executive would find radical change blocked at every turn.

Relax!

So, in an organisation moving into an uncertain future, an early task for the chief executive must be to relax the grip of fear on the minds of individuals. Fortunately, in BT in 1978, the imaginative and moderate leader of the engineers' trade union – Bryan Stanley – was as concerned at the effect of fear on the attitudes of staff as myself. Fear can make reasonable people unpredictable, and only the most tireless of union leaders wishes for that, after he has secured his own personal position. So, in 1978, top management and union together joined in producing a tape and slide presentation that would carry two messages: the new technology is inevitable, and we can win with it. That presentation was shown to each one of the 125,000 technical staff in BT over nine months, and discussed in small groups at the workplace. The presentation was opened by me, as chief executive, together with Bryan Stanley, as General Secretary of the Post Office Engineers' Union; it was put over everywhere at local level, by first line management and union representatives in concert. Its effect was dramatic. In nine months, Bryan Stanley and I agreed that attitudes had been transformed; in my words, "we have driven out fear, only greed remains!" Greed is much easier to handle, and indeed, can even be turned to useful purposes.

Face outwards

With the attitude to change more receptive, the next task is to change the aspect outwards from the bureaucratic concern for internal systems, towards the market place and the value perceived by each customer. By bearing upon a few rules, the new chief executive can change the way in which many thousands of decisions are taken within a traditional structure. For example, in evaluating new technical projects, the traditional concern in BT had been to maximise the perceived Net Present Value. While that seems rational, and indeed laudable, the effect was quite damaging, since a sentence was added to the rule, stipulating, "but you may not count any benefits for which cash is not received by us", or words to that effect. By that apparently innocuous addition, powerful organisational pressure in a monopoly could eject highly desirable features – those elements that bring benefits in customer service or quality, for example, unless they also bring some reduction in maintenance cost or improved operational life. Insisting that the return that counts is the value as perceived by the customer – as Brian Fuller did in the West Midlands Fire Service – is one powerful way in which attitudes in the public service can be turned outwards to the consumer.

In another aspect too, values need to be changed. In a traditional hierarchical structure, the most ringing praise in a personal record is the phrase "so-and-so is an excellent administrator". Where the new chief executive wishes to turn the thoughts of managers outwards, he must attack relentlessly the view that administering procedures rather than achieving results earns the plaudits of the personnel department. Indeed, a leader probably needs to go further, and make it clear that the only opinions on the quality of individuals that matter are those of line managers whose values are clearly linked to achievement and the creation of wealth.

Go for results

There too lies another early task; the key line positions, where responsibility lies for producing the value on which the organisation depends, must be filled by individuals whose attitudes, aspects, and personal criteria are in line with the present and future needs of the enterprise. Students of hierarchies have long observed how thoroughly one misguided hierarch can damage the structure beneath him. One relentlessly introverted bureaucrat at a high level in an organisation can frustrate the attitudes and aspirations of many thousand potentially creative individuals.

So, for five years in BT, I personally vetted all appointments to the top 200 posts in the organisation, choosing, so far as I could judge, achievers, rather than those to whom procedures were all-important. After the first few "excellent administrators" had been turned down, the organisation soon appreciated that those who prospered were leaders, who could manage resources efficiently to achieve results on time. Incidentally, there was an extra benefit: three or four thirty-minute discussions each week with candidates drawn from the middle ranks of the business, provided a vivid insight into where the barriers to achievement lay!

COHERENTLY!

Once the grip of the old hierarchy has been broken, and people placed in positions of authority who are inspired to turn outwards and to achieve results, it does seem to me crucially important that those new aspirations should lie within the broad envelope of corporate strategies, as Templer showed in Malaya. In turbulence, the new strategic statement needs to be very different to those definitive plans developed so impressively by the early business school graduates in the 1960s and 1970s. Then, fortified with a rock-like certainty in mathematical techniques, boldly extrapolating a decade into the future from regression analyses of the past and lines of best fit, strategic plans were packed with numbers. Not only were they misleading, but actively dangerous in implying certainty, when discontinuity was looming.

The ten-year strategic plan that BT published in 1980, after the first stage of delegation had been completed, was quite different. It was primarily conceptual. Stating in words the objectives of the corporation, it described the logic of the new competitive market place, and of the broad strategic movements that would give the corporation the best chance of success, however the wild cards turned out. Numbers were used, for example in describing the quality of present performance in relation to the past and to other businesses elsewhere – emphasising where improvements were needed, rather than parading signals for self-congratulation. Numbers were used, but to define targets for the improvement in service and in the capability of the network by specific dates; thirty major cities linked to the Integrated Services Digital Network by 1986, five million customers on System X by 1990, for example.

That plan, in sharp distinction to earlier secrecy, was published in an edition of 40,000 copies, one for each manager within the corporation, and others for the consumer groups and those outside with an interest in the development of the industry. The purpose of that document was to create throughout the business a conceptual framework within which the personal initiatives of many thousands of individuals could be caused to converge – by the spontaneous goodwill of the newly freed managers, rather than by specific direction from the top.

In BT, to that conceptual structure was added also an architecture for technology. In the development of System X, it was quite clear that standards would need to define the interfaces between system elements, so that each could be developed separately. It was clear that the elements of software also needed defined interfaces, so that separate teams of engineers could work independently, knowing that their work would fit when the system was brought together.

It also became clear more generally, that as the initiative for information technology projects was moved out into the operational areas of the business, a new way of working was needed if standards were to hold firm when initiative had passed to non-specialists. We adopted a practice from the military. I called it the "cap-badge" principle; it stipulated that the Director of Data Processing, as he was named at that time, had direct authority over information professionals on professional matters – including training and technical standards. However, on operational issues, including the priorities of work, the authority would lie with the line manager concerned. Thus the computing executives who were assigned to the Prestel team came under the command of its leader. In just the same way, the Signal Officer-in-Chief of the British Army has professional command over all signallers, who wear the Mercury cap-badge, while for tasks they come under the line authority of the brigade or divisional commander to whom they are assigned. IBM follows a similar rule for its own computing requirements; 98 per cent of its information specialists are assigned to the line command of operating divisions, close to the market place, concerned with creating wealth rather than corporate monuments, but under the professional leadership of the Director of Information Systems.

In moving from the tightly controlled hierarchic pyramids of the past towards a new agility, we still have much to learn. In 1988, fierce criticism was levelled in a McKinsey report for the British NEDO, at companies in the electronics industry, suggesting that while they had decentralised decision making, that devolution of authority had not been matched by a cohesive strategy; abdication rather than delegation, as the old phrase has it. There is the new paradox from which success must flow: empower the individual, but within a fruitful vector.

WHERE ARE THE LEADERS?

In one other practical way, a military precedent helped in the transformation of BT. In 1980, I spoke in a public lecture[4] of Napoleon's technique for developing the leaders for his *Grand Armée*. He used the *corps d'élite*. Starting in 1800 with a guard some 2,000 strong, he used that body over the next fifteen years to transform the quality of the whole army. He brought individuals of promising quality into the guard for a limited period, where he could develop their morale and skills under his own personal supervision. Many were then moved out to commands in line regiments, carrying with them the spirit that their service in the *corps d'élite* had given them. Others were retained, and the Imperial Guard itself grew to 50,000 strong by 1812 and the advance into Russia; finally over 100,000 men were included.

In 1980, BT was able to report to a military audience that four such bodies had been established, in which the new junior leadership of the corporation could be formed. The International Executive, Prestel, Telconsult, and the System X development team were each given a freedom in organisation still deemed impracticable for the remaining 200,000. The leader of each of those four units was given free poaching rights in recruiting staff, which gave the incidental benefit, for a new chief executive, of identifying talent hidden in the depths of the organisation. Later, many of the most successful appointments at senior level were drawn from these pools, where talent had been coupled with the spirit to achieve.

In moving from the predictable and protected markets of yesterday, managers in every sort of business – public and private – must expect to find turbulence. Turbulence that brings with it constantly changing terrain and the need for agility; when that agility and the creative power of many individuals can be harnessed towards corporate objectives, the new turbulence can bring great opportunities for progress. Indeed, the confident and skilled leader will welcome tumult as opening opportunities for the talented, while confusing the humdrum. Jungle war in Malaya was not only successful, but notably less horrible than four years and several million casualties in the mud of Flanders. The bold and the vigorous will find exhilaration in the new freedoms, and bring new wealth, if they can achieve that fruitful balance of individual initiative and broad strategy that General Templer displayed so finely in the testing climate of a guerrilla campaign. It should be easier for us!

NOTES

1 Siegfried Sassoon, "Base Details", in *The War Poems of Siegfried Sassoon*, ed. Rupert Hart-Davies (Faber and Faber, London), p. 198.
2 A. P. Wavell, *The Palestine Campaigns* (Constable, London, 1928).
3 Noel Barber, *The War of the Running Dogs* (Collins, London, 1971).
4 Peter Benton, 'Managing the telecommunications revolution', *Journal of the Royal Signals Institution* (1981).

5

THE NEW LODESTAR

CERTAIN, BUT WRONG

"I WISH I was as cocksure of anything" said Lord Melbourne, "as Tom Macaulay is of everything." Known for his phenomenal memory, Lord Macaulay was reputed to remember whole passages word perfectly, years after a single reading. In the stable world in which he grew up – socially stable as Jane Austen depicts, despite the Napoleonic wars – that certainty of recall gave him an assurance about the future exasperating to the more tentative man. Strong logic applied to certain knowledge may give rather unsafe predictions, if the world is being turned upside down. In the political turmoil of a Britain adjusting to the revolution of the 1832 Reform Bill, Melbourne's open mind was perhaps more appropriate in a Prime Minister. Certainly, Queen Victoria was fortunate in finding such a guide for her first years on the throne.

The end of our own feudal period was marked too by men with strong certainties, derived from an undoubting knowledge of the past, analysed into predictions through the new statistical techniques. In the 1960s, antique silver, British agricultural land, and the business strategies of conglomerates like Ling Tempco Vaught and Litton Industries seemed so assured in their certain progression that they attracted huge followings, soon to be disappointed.

Of course it had all been seen before, in the seventeenth century for example. Then, the normally prudent Dutch allowed their rational instincts to run away with them, in the remarkable tulip-omania boom. When a single bulb of "Viceroy" could fetch 2,500 silver florins, and the red and white "Semper Augustus" twice as much, with a new carriage and pair of horses thrown in, faith in extrapolating from a trend had reached an impressive influence. When the crash came, in February 1637, prices fell 90 per cent but at least the flowers were there to enjoy. Eighty years later, a similar mania developed in England, for company stocks, under the influence of the South Sea Bubble. At its height, James Puckle floated a company to make his machine gun, firing round bullets at Christians and square ones at Turks, patented in May 1718. A wit immune from the prevailing folly wrote:[1]

> A rare invention to Destroy the Crowd
> Of Fools at home, instead of Foes abroad:
> Fear not, my Friends, this Terrible Machine,
> They're only Wounded that have Shares therein.

Folly, pure folly; and yet, when the Bubble burst in 1720, people did not ruefully laugh at themselves for their credulity and greed, but turned with fury on a few designated scapegoats. Perhaps that is what politicians are for – lightning conductors for public disenchantment – though F. S. Oliver, in *The Endless Adventure*,[2] gave them the more noble metaphor of the mongoose, attacking the cobra adventurer like Kipling's Riki Tiki Tavi!

It seems all the more surprising that, 250 years on, a new era of crazy certainties could have gathered speed. The common cause, across a wide front of follies, lay in confidence that the past could be extrapolated to the future; that a certain knowledge of what had been could, by undeniable processes of logic, be a sure guide to the future. Well of course, it could, provided that everything else remained the same. Induction, inferring general principles from separate observations, may be a powerful means for deriving the laws of science, but those *laws* may not be immutable laws of nature, and only hold good while the conditions that influenced the observed phenomena remain unchanged. St Augustine's "quid metiatur non erit" ("what may be measured will not be") seems rather relevant in turbulence.

Everywhere the examples are there: trends of solid measurable facts run true for a time, and then go haywire, as conditions change. Take the art world, for example. Today, as we are encouraged to invest in pictures and objects of *virtu*, it might be as well to look into the history of that trade in *The Economics of Taste*.[3] First published in the 1960s, and tracing the sale value of particular objects over several centuries, that book shows that it is far from safe to extrapolate a future price for an object by studying its past record. A portrait by Raeburn sells to Duveen in 1911 and then to Knoedler in 1926 for £24,000, and reappears thirty years later in New York at a fifth of the price, in currency that has halved its value. Mezzotints had two great booms – in the 1880s, and in the 1920s – and today are neglected. Those were changes in taste. The boom in Georgian silver, that peaked around 1970, had different causes. There the price surge was created by the operation of the market itself, with speculators crowding into a limited supply. As they fed their enthusiasm with the higher prices that their own competition generated, that trend seemed to prove for a time that extrapolation was valid. Old English silver, chosen because its authenticity was *guaranteed* by hallmarks, and the immortal observation "they don't make any more of it", seemed just the sort of tradable commodity in which those ignorant of the art world could invest safely. If the forces at work had been understood, the fragility of the phenomenon would have warned that the trend was likely to be temporary. Other convincing sequences have not yet experienced their discontinuity!

The boom in the 1960s in British agricultural land, which led some notably numerate individuals to make huge investments in thousands of acres, was a quite different phenomenon, though "they don't make any more of it" seemed equally applicable. The price per acre of land at that time, although perhaps more obviously linked to economic value than Georgian silver, was nevertheless far higher than the value of the produce justified. Few bothered to ask why. If they had, they might have observed that agricultural land was treated very favourably in calculating estate duties on the death of wealthy individuals. Whereas other assets suffered tax at 80 per cent, holders of agricultural land were able to leave one-half of that wealth to their heirs. In those circumstances it was not surprising that the price of land should be several times higher than the output would justify. When that particular tax provision was changed, prices collapsed. Another linear trend that behaved strangely when a latent factor emerged.

EXPLODED PRECEPTS

I can well remember a discussion in New York during the late 1960s with the chief executive of one conglomerate, and architect of the amazing growth in its share price. I was impressed then by the mathematical inevitability of his strategic formula. He put it thus, as I recall:

If you can achieve a price earnings ratio for your shares of forty, use those shares to buy dull companies with reliable earnings, with a PE perhaps of eight or ten. As you consolidate their earnings with your own, your profits will grow five times faster than you increase your issued capital; earnings per share will rise steadily, and numerate analysts will puff up the price of your stock.

It seemed, from the lips of the master, a system of beautiful inevitability. The acquisitions that your share price made possible, helped in turn to maintain the value of your shares – and thus to add more acquisitions still. Unfortunately there was a flaw, small at first but growing until it brought the whole scheme crashing down. As the size of the group grew, the volume of new acquisitions needed to keep the share price rising grew even faster. At the same time, the ramshackle empire became increasingly unwieldy and difficult to manage; those reliable profits wobbled. When the crash came, the price earnings ratio fell from forty to eight in a few weeks, and the party was over. Another linear trend bit the dust.

In Britain, the electronics industry has seen radical changes in the formulae for calculating price, that invalidate straightforward projections of profitability. The tale is a cautionary one, and deserves a full explanation. In the 1960s, a British defence contractor did a terrible thing. Ferranti produced some new equipment for the military at a lower cost than either they or the Ministry of Aviation had estimated. Their "excess profit" caused a scandal of nuclear proportions.

Since then, for twenty years British government departments have bought on the infamous cost-plus rules. So that profit as a percentage of costs should never be embarrassing, that ratio was fixed by a process known as the Treasury Profit Formula. In 1980, for example, a manufacturer was allowed to keep 13.5 per cent on top of costs incurred, whatever those costs might be. This system, so typically bureaucratic and comfortable for Organisation Man, was pernicious in several respects. First, it encouraged under-capitalisation; if, for example, you could turn over your capital employed three times in a year, a 13.5 per cent mark up on cost became a healthy 40 per cent return on capital, with negligible risk. Sadly, that drive to economise on capital kept factories labour intensive, suppliers waiting for their money, and production machines too crowded with routine work to allow swift intro-duction of new models. Secondly, since research and development on agreed projects was paid for with a 100 per cent mark up on cost, speculative science had little attraction. Indeed, if new technology threatened to reduce costs, it was financially unattractive to the manufacturer; better to negotiate a new research contract, to "seize the full opportunities available"! Meanwhile, the traditional product would continue to generate its risk free return. Organisation Men elsewhere loved the system too. Fortunately, after years of lost opportunity, the damaging effects have been recognised widely, and that method has been driven out of use; only a fraction of British defence procurement is now on this basis, and the Pentagon is expelling it too.

Clearly, the research programmes, organisation structures, and decision rules developed under that bizarre regime cannot safely be carried forward into the New Age. And even though many man-agers were aware of the fallacies inherent in the old rules, and did thrust forward with technical and marketing initiatives, irrespective of short-term financial advantage, it cannot be safe in logic to project the financial performance of such companies as though nothing had changed. For the best, no doubt sales and profit will grow faster, as new technology is used boldly for commercial advantage. For those who cannot throw off the old practices, first the plateau, and then the slide downhill.

STEERING BY YOUR WAKE?

So, steering by your wake, in the American phrase, has proved dangerous and expensive, long before the revolution caused by information technology and the dismantling of market barriers. To borrow an expression from mathematics, the apparently simple linear equation that seems to describe a complex of factors almost certainly contains latent terms, with high orders of multiplication. While society is feudal, and markets regulated, the variables in those terms may be constrained, and therefore insignificant; when those constraints are removed, the smooth flow of the stream breaks into turbulence.

Well, if one may not steer by the wake, and the future is certainly turbulent, what is one to do? What star should we steer by?

Whose values?

The New Age calls for new attitudes. The backward-looking and the introverted will not set the right course. The answer must surely be to look forwards and outwards, towards the customer and what he will need when you are ready to supply. Judging what constitutes value in the eyes of the recipient of a product or service, must be the best guide to using the new technologies fruitfully, and to anticipating the most dangerous actions of competitors. Those values, however, may be quite different to the qualities traditionally perceived within an organisation, may vary from time to time, will not be the same for all customers, and can be quite different elsewhere in the world. There will be few absolutes; when customers have choice, they will go for the option that gives the best value in their particular circumstances, when they wish to choose.

It is all a far cry from the old certainties. In the early 1970s, I became chairman of an engineering company renowned for a particular design of valve, much used in the process plant industry. I was puzzled to find that in Europe a German copyist was charging 10 per cent more for a very similar product, and winning orders. That competitor was particularly successful with turnkey contractors, who were committed to deliver working plants on time. I was intrigued; in true traditional aspects of value, low price and technical quality, my company was at least as good as its competitor. But when I explored further, and talked with some of those contractors directly, the cause of our discomfiture became plain. For them, the late arrival of any component – particularly if it delayed the commissioning date – could be extremely expensive; penalty payments could exceed the cost of all the valves purchased. As one contractor put it, "there's a saying in my firm, that your company's valves are always the last bits of kit on site; we couldn't afford them if they were free!" For a customer in those circumstances, reliability of delivery was a crucial aspect of value; without it, price and technical quality could not by themselves make the product attractive.

For customers in different circumstances, the reliability of delivery may be much less significant. For distributors, the economic calculation was relatively straightforward. Unreliable delivery could be offset by higher stockholding, with that cost balanced against other commercial considerations, including price and volume discounts. The particular circumstances of individual customers determined the relative value to them of different aspects of my company's service.

Sudhir Mulji, a leading Indian shipowner, once chairman of that country's consortium negotiating the transport of iron ore, has an instructive tale. Negotiations with the British Steel Corporation were traditional; hard bargaining on shipping rates, down to market levels. The Japanese steel men were rather unusual; they agreed on terms 15 per cent above the norm, but insisted on rigorous specification of arrival times, accurate to the hour. It was not that they were ignorant of the Indian costs – Mulji was later shown an accurate and detailed analysis – but rather that they knew what really mattered in their terms. Instructive, as another aspect of the Japanese concern for quality, and good evidence too that they handle their affairs in the round, with the procurement and transport specialists well briefed on the broader economic consequences of their particular task. Would that all were so! Sometimes the stringencies seem hard to understand, as Allied-Signal found in selling brake pads to Toyota: Paint them? Why, they will never be seen once they are fitted. Still, done to standard, they won 20 per cent of the business, and went on to be specified for the joint venture plant of Toyota and General Motors in Fremont, California, as David Montgomery of Stanford reports in his 1989 research paper.[4]

Especially confusing to some traditional engineers, is the differing view that particular customers may take of the value of engineering quality, in its various aspects. In 1975, the British Design Council reverse-engineered, at my request, two air conditioning products, one British and one German. They reported that the British system was excellently designed, with each element properly sized in relation to the others, according to traditional criteria of elegant engineering. The German equipment did not pass those criteria at all; the heat exchanger, the compressor, and other elements were mismatched in capacity in a way that any engineer dedicated to traditional professional attitudes would have found deplorable. However, the components were standard. In the more elegant British design, most were special to that particular equipment. On traditional introverted criteria, the first system was clearly more excellent. However, to owners of property in, shall we say, the Persian Gulf, where spares are hard to come by and maintenance engineers relatively inexperienced, the inelegant system that was easiest to keep in service was seen to deliver better value, and was bought.

Take another example. Lotus, now part of General Motors, make high performance motor cars for the luxury market. As one executive put it, "we worry about product warranties too, but with rather different priorities." While traditionally motor manufacturers have been most concerned to avoid the product faults that cost most to rectify after delivery, Lotus point out that in a luxury motor car, stray oil on a hinge – no great crime to the traditional engineer – could damage the perception of value in a customer as much as a mechanical failure. If a new coat or an expensive piece of luggage is marked, that customer perceives a destruction of wealth.

Another illustration, to make the point in another context. Many users of personal computers have found that their equipment has given mechanical or software trouble at some time. Most take such glitches with equanimity – unless the fault wipes the computer's memory; losing many hours of work can be hard to forgive. Some faults are venal, some are deadly sins; the prudent designer concerned with value perceived by the customer should judge well where his priorities lie. The best Japanese companies have an economic formula; count the cost of product failure to the customer before you decide on the optimum balance between quality and price. You may then find you get both benefits; high quality can be cheaper to make, certainly where computer software is involved!

Some great corporations are sufficiently sympathetic to the bewilderment of a new customer in a first encounter with complicated equipment, to write handbooks specific to the particular variant that a customer has bought. General Motors do this in their Detroit plant. Once the last variant has been committed to the car moving along the assembly line, a handbook is produced from data in the computer system for that particular product, leaving out the information on options that were not chosen. How strange, then, that IBM should offer its new PS/2 hard disk personal computer with a handbook that also describes the operating procedures for two preceding models. That seems an example of the introverted view of Organisation Man still rampant; a little effort is saved, but a lot of customers become quite confused, and resent the loss of time. It may be that their perception of value in an otherwise superb product is materially damaged by ambiguity in what was, no doubt, limpidly clear to the IBMer who approved the guide. So, creating value in the eyes of the customer requires a sympathetic understanding of what the particular customer, however ignorant in your terms, will value or regard as damaging to his or her interests.

ASK, OR UNDERSTAND?

With new technology capable of offering so much variety, how can those characteristics of a product or service that may be valuable in the customer's eyes best be judged? Probably not by asking the direct question! Famous in commercial history is the case of the Ford Edsel. Flushed with enthusiasm for market research and the "Customer is King" theme, the Ford Motor Company set out not long after World War II, determined to design the motor car the customer really wanted. The result was the Edsel, the most famous flop in automobile history. What went wrong? First, I suggest, the customers, when asked in their questionnaires which features they valued – trim, stoplights like rocket motors, and the rest – fed back to the researchers the attitudes that Ford's own advertising had instilled in their perceptions. Secondly, when the car appeared on the market, several years later, they had changed their minds. Two fundamental flaws in the process: a misunderstanding about true values, and a failure to aim ahead of the flying bird! For twenty more years Ford produced *committee cars*, as CEO Donald Petersen told the Stanford Design Forum in 1988; then came a recognition that intuition and emotion have their role in marketing and corporate strategy – and we saw the Taurus, launched to success in 1985. "Informed instinct" was a phrase Kazuyoshi Ishizaka, President of Japan's Kenwood Corporation, used on the same occasion. Sardonically, Galbraith had this to say in *The Affluent Society*,[5] "Some have even pointed out that in the same week the Russians launched the first earth satellite we launched a magnificent selection of car models including the uniquely elegant Edsel"!

Another large corporation changed earlier than Ford. Rolls Royce, after the catharsis of bankruptcy in 1971, purged its own faith in internal values and adopted a more outward looking approach. Take designing a new civil aero-engine, for example; the Tay, happily much in demand for medium-sized airliners working from airports near city centres, owed its success to forethought and empathy. Recognising that it takes two to three years longer to develop a new engine than to develop the air frame that will carry it, the Rolls team knew that a direct question to its customers would not necessarily give the right answer; they did not need yet to make up their mind about their product; Rolls Royce did. So the specification, if the new engine were to be successful, depended upon judging what the air frame makers would value when they did come to their own decision time. And that value depended, of course, on the perceived values of their customers in turn – the aircraft operators.

As for Rolls Royce in the late 1970s, so too for most businesses in other industries; in deciding what you will offer, imagine yourself in the circumstances of your customer, and then look back and judge what you can do that will best meet those perceived values. Making that judgement well demands technical skills, engineering and commercial, but also the human qualities of sympathy and imagination. If those judgements are made soundly, drawing on the best of your own capabilities to deliver the greatest value perceived by your customer, the wealth created will sharpen your competitive edge. Soundly pursued, that principle must be the surest guide in a turbulent age.

Well, that may be all very well for those who work in the trading sector of the economy, in a competitive market place where economic value can be proved. What is one to do in the public service, or in those remaining parts of the economy where choice is constrained? The issue is alive: customers for those monopoly products and services have had their expectations whetted by their new richness of choice elsewhere; the resigned respect for bureaucratic authority has not survived the availability of choice in the market place. Public servants or monopolists have found that the penalties of failing to judge value through the customer's criteria can be painful, even though they may not go bankrupt – although that too can be a threat, when the regulatory system allows the aggrieved customer to hit back hard. AT & T's Californian operation in the late 1970s found angry regulators refusing adequate rate increases, and so damaging profits and destroying the bond rating; that made it pay attention! London Transport's perceived unconcern about passenger safety cost two leading executives their jobs. The managers of British Telecom have had to face taunts that cannot have been pleasant. It was certainly not agreeable in 1987, for a former chief executive to hear that company's quality of service and customer relations ridiculed by actors in Singapore, to strong applause from an appreciative audience; the sympathy of the chairman of Singapore Telecom was hard to bear!

WHO ARE THE WEALTH CREATORS?

John Stuart Mill wrote "Money, being the instrument of an important public and private purpose, is rightly regarded as wealth; but everything else which serves any human purpose, and which nature does not afford gratuitously, is wealth also."[6] While Mill, later in his book, takes a more restricted view of wealth,[7] his broader definition, cited in the Oxford English Dictionary, seems to me to expound a valuable concept: a concept that can bring management of public service and monopoly enterprises into close harmony with the more obvious requirements of success in the competitive trading sector. Companies that face competitors have to turn introverted eyes outwards, and expel bureaucratic concern for following internal procedures. If they do not, their customers will find others who will. Large trading corporations protected by patents, or by sheer power in the market place, may be given a year or two to change their ways, but change they must or face extinction. In the public service, and in monopolies, the pressures for change may seem oblique, and more remote. However, their leaders too need to define a new guiding principle, because steering by the wake can cause customer anger, all the greater for being thwarted for longer. John Stuart Mill's first theme brings that guiding light; it was confirmed in 1883, when Henry Sidgwick's phrase "value in use" gave the essential criterion of wealth.[8]

If then it is sound to say that wealth is created whenever a product or service is enjoyed, whose value to the recipient is greater than the cost of resources consumed in its production, then almost everyone at work can be a wealth creator. It is just that when the value of a product is recognised in a market transaction, the amount of wealth created can be measured; where no money changes hands, or where the customer has no choice, it is more difficult to tell how well you are performing. Surely, though, it is more important to create wealth than to measure it? Adopting that principle can turn the eyes of bureaucrats outwards, to the great benefit of us all.

That theme, embracing natural assets too, gives common cause to leaders in every sort of activity; the techniques that work best, where wealth creation can be proved, may be just as valuable when the wealth is enjoyed but cannot be measured. That attitude, with its concern for the benefit given rather than the reward extracted, seems the key to a benign transition from monopoly towards a market in which the consumer has real choice – whether that monopoly is held through state law, or a fact of famine. Creating wealth is for everyone.

Notes

1 John Ellis, *The Social History of the Machine Gun* (Croom Helm, London, 1975), p. 14.

2 F. S. Oliver, *The Endless Adventure*, vol. iii (Macmillan, London, 1935), p. 159.
3 Gerald Reitlinger, *The Economics of Taste*, vol. iii (Hacker, New York, 1982), p. 416.
4 David B. Montgomery, "Understanding the Japanese as customers, competitors, and collaborators", Research Paper, Stanford University, April 1989.
5 J. K. Galbraith, *The Affluent Society* (Hamish Hamilton, London, 1958).
6 John Stuart Mill, *Principles of Political Economy*, vol. i (Parker, London, 1848), p. 8.
7 Ibid., vol. i, pp. 55–66.
8 Henry Sidgwick, *The Principles of Political Economy* (Macmillan, London, 1883), pp. 70–92.

6

PUBLIC AND PRIVATE

WHY BUREAUCRATS?

OF course, bureaucracy can foster wealth. The great Chinese Renaissance of the eleventh century was made possible by the Mandarin structure of the Sung emperors. Jacques Gernet describes the achievement convincingly in *History of Chinese Civilisation*.[1] After the fragmentation and petty tyrannies at the end of the Tang dynasty, the new bureaucracy moved swiftly to create the framework within which prosperity could be created, in the forty years after 1000 AD. First, a single copper coinage throughout the Empire, then the state expanded the unofficial financial systems of the wealthy merchants and financiers, printing bank notes and creating negotiable financial instruments. From the first issue in Szechwan in 1024 to the fourteenth century, certificates of credit, flying money (*fei-ch'ien*), the cheque, the promissory note, and the bill of exchange made possible an extraordinary increase in trade, both internal and across the seas.

This famous civil service, an inspiration for the British reforms in the nineteenth century, established a structure that set the rules for every aspect of Chinese life, staffed by men of high calibre. Never many, the Mandarin could only be appointed after successfully passing public examinations – intriguingly, for the highest grade skill in poetry was mandatory. The Sung emperors had their great civil servants. Wang An-Shih, for example,[2] created fiscal policy, administrative rules, and controls over the military that were put in place over thirty years in the middle of the eleventh century. The control of fraud, state loans to counter usury, and the stabilisation of agricultural markets all tended towards the settled and universal structure that enabled China to reach the highest point in its history, whether measured in terms of economic prosperity or artistic creation.

In the nineteenth century, Britain too had its reformers. Sir Charles Trevelyan, married, incidentally, to Macaulay's sister, brought some of his brother-in-law's certainty towards the structure of the Home Civil Service. From his power base in the Treasury,[3] he followed in Wang An-Shih's footsteps, expelling the place-men and sinecurists who made the organs of government so inefficient and subject to improper pressure during the Georgian era. As in Sung China, men of high intellectual quality were attracted to the service, and selected through tough public examinations – examinations that gave the credit to skill in turning Latin hexameters that would have been awarded a candidate Mandarin for his understanding of the nine classics, published by imperial command between the years 932 and 952 AD.

The Chinese achievement is all the more remarkable when one considers the corrupt and restrictive systems of their predecessors and contemporaries on the other side of the world, in Rome and Byzantium. In sharp contrast to the emperors of the Sung dynasty, who voluntarily confined themselves to the role of constitutional monarch, relying on the public service of their brilliant and educated civil servants, the Roman emperors were, with few exceptions, tyrants. Their civil service was drawn from Rome's slave population, wholly dependent on imperial favour; powerful public servants showed little concern for the public good in the pursuit of personal wealth, once they had secured personal freedom from slavery. That good man, the younger Pliny, gives a flavour of the Roman loathing for that particular type of bureaucrat. Writing to his friend Montanus, he says,[4] "you would laugh to see the monument erected to Pallas on the Via Tiburtina. That such honours should be thrown away on such filth, how dare that villain accept them or reject." Still, the Roman Empire continued to work, and its economy to function. But, as Edward Gibbon has shown,[5] the government system tended inexorably to lose its effectiveness, as the people saw successive emperors deposed by assassination or military putsch, often in response to fury of the kind that Pliny shows in his letter to Montanus, and Juvenal in his satires.

Constantinople was more orderly, but its bureaucracy gave the word Byzantine the sense "intricate, complicated, inflexible, rigid and unyielding", listed in the Oxford Dictionary. In the Middle Ages the city was said to be "the paradise of monopoly, privilege, and protection", with labour, industry and finance closely regulated. Not surprisingly, as Charles Diehl points out in the *Cambridge Medieval History*,[6] the Venetians seized the commerce: "Byzantium shewed scanty interest in opening commercial channels and conducting her own export trade, but took pride in seeing all the world meet on the shores of the Bosphorous." Is there, perhaps, a resemblance to the financial market of the City of London?

FRAMEWORKS FOR THE IMAGINATION

Structure is important to the process of creation. It is surely no accident that the verse form of the sonnet has proved the vehicle for some of the most beautiful lyrics in the English language. Shakespeare found that the rules constraining him to fourteen lines of ten syllables each, with rhymes in a special order, made possible imagination and verbal beauty. Edith Sitwell wrote of another fertile genius that the free form of blank verse "would have been impossible to a poet of Pope's tiny and weak body; but the stopped heroic couplet, with its sustaining rhymes, its outward cage (though that cage holds within it all the waves, and the towers, and the gulfs of the world), this was born to be his measure".[7] Every line we have of Virgil's verse is a polished hexameter. Edmund Spenser, although he invented his own structure for *The Faerie Queen*, held to it for several thousand verses.

In architecture, the wonderful variety of renaissance buildings was created within a structure of rules, defined for us first by Vitruvius in the reign of Augustus, and then interpreted for modern times by the Venetian architect Palladio and his successors. Throughout Europe in the eighteenth century, country builders, far away from capital cities and the centres of taste, could design delightful houses, relying on the rules of proportion set out in the handbooks of Serlio, de l'Orme or Batty Langley. Turning to our times, can we say that architects have designed better buildings after they jettisoned the precepts of the past? Perhaps the great artists with natural genius have succeeded in forming a new language for their art – rather as Spenser developed a new prosody for. Intriguingly, that most commercial of all American cities, Chicago, provided the clients for three of the great, creative architects of this century: Frank Lloyd Wright, Louis Sullivan, and Mies Van der Rohe. Peter Smithson, although classed by some as a leading neo-brutalist, built the lovely Economist building in St James's Street, London, reminiscent for me of a Venetian stage set of the sixteenth century, illustrated in Sebastiano Serlio's *Architettura*, for example, or my 1567 *Vitruvius*, with its woodcuts after Palladio.

Structure is crucial to creation. Indeed, when in 1980 BT was commissioning its new headquarters building, within sight of St Paul's Cathedral, I asked Theo Crosby RA for his advice on how a client should behave. The answer was clear: "Create constraints". Even arbitrary constraints would, in his view, provide the skeleton upon which a creative mind could work. Perhaps fortunately, the city planners responded to that need! Height, volume, a view of the drum of St Paul's dome from two specified points, and street frontages on all sides were their constraints; we banned a monolith. Some say the result has been a success. Certainly, the streets and squares of London, designed under the fire and building regulations of the eighteenth century, show a variety combined with harmony that makes them most agreeable to human beings of very different cultures.

So, if structure is necessary to the imagination, why does it sometimes stifle? Perhaps where it binds too closely *how* something should be done, rather than define the crucial elements of the outward relationship. In advanced technology, the art has been to establish international standards that specify the necessary interfaces and interconnections, but leave the details optional within each module. The new European standards in telecommunications and computing try to follow that rule; the goal, independent invention by thousands of engineers and scientists, with assured interworking of their products throughout a large market and across national frontiers. The worldwide drive towards Open Systems Interconnect (OSI) standards has a further objective: that structure is there to open the market for terminals to everyone, on a level footing, relaxing the tight grip of IBM with its proprietary SNA network architecture. Intriguingly the US Department of Defense is a strong supporter, to increase its choice of suppliers and to make inter-connection easier with the civil and military systems of allies. Now IBM too is within the OSI fold.

Structure can influence creativity in another way also. Monoliths tend to choose massive solutions, if only because the task of man-aging many small activities centrally can be daunting. So most large investment funds shy away from the entrepreneur and his small but troublesome affairs though some, like the two Prudentials in the United States and in Britain, have set up special offshoots for that specific purpose. That is why the Business Expansion Scheme was introduced by the British government, giving tax breaks to private individuals investing in start-up companies.

Monoliths can inhibit valuable technology as well. In Britain, the huge Central Electricity Generating Board has naturally favoured huge power stations. The new freedom for private power generation gives an opportunity to the small gas turbine combined-cycle gen-erating units that just would not have been used in the monolith days. With 80 per cent thermal efficiency achievable where waste heat can be used locally for climate control, twice the yield of traditional power stations, they deserve to succeed, but had to wait for the change in organisational scale.

In central government, the reorganisation of the British Civil Service in the obscurely named *Next Steps* programme opens up some intriguing new possibilities. With dozens of functions hived off into executive agencies and huge bureaucracies like the Training Agency with its £3 billion a year to spend, divided among 100 or so Training and Enterprise Councils run by local businessmen, the scale of government bodies is changing dramatically. Those changes multiply the points for initiative, and open new chances for ideas stifled by scale.

PUBLIC INTEREST, PRIVATE PROFIT

The Chinese Mandarins of the Sung era, while they created the framework within which entrepreneurs could prosper, were profoundly wary of the breed. Constantly, they were concerned lest greed and irresponsible objectives should cause individuals or groups to damage the stability on which they depended, in search of short-term or personal gains. The twelfth-century ironmaster Wang Ko prospered in south central China from an economic base of a tree-covered mountainside which provided the charcoal for his furnaces. Wang Ko challenged the authority of the local officials, and attacked the town in which they were based. He was executed. On a wider scale, and more generally, the disturbing influence of maritime traders led the Mandarins of the early Ming period to forbid the construction of seagoing ships altogether. That ban on overseas trade followed thirty years of naval power in the China Seas and the Indian Ocean under Admiral Cheng Ho.[8] To the Mandarins of the Chinese Renaissance, no commercial wealth justified disturbance of the imperial peace. It will be interesting to see if similar con-siderations influence the Chinese attitude to Hong Kong.

How would those old Mandarins have reacted to the behaviour of those public service enterprises in Britain that have recently been returned to private hands? Where the customer has choice, there is always protection against high-handed behaviour: shop somewhere else. The problem comes, though, when a monopoly – whether natural or contrived – is run on lines other than those concerned with service to the public, as the United States learned unforgettably in the last years of the nineteenth century. William Henry Van-derbilt's "The Public be damned" and J. P. Morgan's Northern Securities Company, with its near total monopoly of railroads in the northwest, brought the dead letter of the Sherman Anti-Trust Act to life. Why? Because no sooner in possession of a monopoly, than those financiers abused it. As the Supreme Court heard, sidings were discontinued, trains ran late, and rates were set to rise. For-tunately for the United States, the first modern monopolists were among the greediest, fortified by the dictum that "a man may do what he will, with his own"! That outrageous challenge did the trick; in 1902, twelve years after the Sherman Act became law, it was first made to bite, and now any operator of a private monopoly in that country knows that the first economic law is to please the customer – or at least the consumerists!

That experience may yet prove relevant again, as Eastern Europe recovers in a start from forty years of planned economy and endemic shortage. All very well for western businessmen to preach the virtues of pricing for what the market will bear, but what if you are the only baker in town? Russia's first rash of co-operatives under *perestroika* showed just how unpopular such aggression can be, when consumers have no choice in essentials. De facto monopolies are no easier than those established by law.

CRITERIA FOR VICTORY

In Britain in the 1980s, many such monopolies have passed from public ownership into the heady freedoms of the stock exchange. Certainly privatisation has stimulated the desire of those managers to win; but it has changed the criteria for victory. Not for long, however; BT, which thought, after privatisation in 1984, that the criteria for victory lay in the growth of profits and the pursuit of business customers, who alone had a competitor to choose from, was soon aware of retribution. In just three years, a leading Conservative Member of Parliament could say to me that BT was the second most loathed organisation in Britain, closely following the IRA! If the British system of regulating monopolies had given public opinion an easier form of expression, no doubt the message would have been received earlier. But whether in Sung China or in a modern state, abuse of monopoly power will bring its retribution. Strange that so many exemplary public servants should stray into antisocial behaviour. Perhaps that contempt for the merchant classes noticed in Chinese Mandarins has its parallel in today's civil servants. Certainly I found among able managers in the old telecommunications service a disturbing belief that private enterprise was run by rogues constrained only by the law. Perhaps that attitude has led some privatised public servants into a quite unhelpful idea of the behaviour appropriate to their new circumstances!

British Telecom, for example – and there are others – showed that its people could be quite piratical. Complaints lodged in 1986 with the industry's regulator alleged that BT's local managers were denying prompt telephone service to customers who had chosen to buy from a competitor equipment that could have been supplied by them – even though the products were identical, and both originally sold by BT's own wholesaler, British Telecom Consumer Products. Strangely, top managers defended that behaviour for months. And then again, the strange affair of the quality of service reports. Each quarter, since 1980, the achievement in quality of service had been published, region by region throughout the country. Those figures, in showing customer and staff alike what progress or failures had been made in the frequency of faults, speed of repair, and in the operation of the automatic network, provided an impulse to improvement, or at least a hint that somebody noticed. Then, in 1984 came the announcement; no more quality of service statistics will be published, since they contain sensitive information of value to a competitor! Not surprisingly, the quality of service fell steadily from then on, until massive protests and those jokes in Singapore and elsewhere brought home the message. The most dangerous enemy of freedom is the person who abuses it.

PLEASING THE VOTER

It has been said more than once that the best regulation of a private monopoly is that which brings pressures to bear that are similar to those of an effective market place. Easily said, but more difficult to achieve.

In the United States, with its long tradition of separate powers and state autonomy, the regulatory system was developed primarily in response to the predator capitalists of the nineteenth century. Private monopolies are regulated throughout the Union on two general principles: the return on capital from monopoly operations should be reasonable, and prices should be set each year by a body responsive to elected government. That system can produce some absurd economic effects, but it certainly has shown the monopolists what they must do to prosper: they must please their customers.

The economic disadvantages of the American system were not so obvious while the economy moved forward in a steady, predictable way, and technology changed relatively slowly. Since regulation allows the monopolist a reasonable rate of return, that implies determining what capital can properly be counted, and what operating costs can be accepted. Those issues give rise to the greatest complexities when technology is changing, and have certainly helped multiply the number of lawyers employed on both sides – regulator and regulated.

Whenever I see some aspect of a United States utility where the economics puzzle me, I ask the confidential question, "Is it in the rate base?" Because, of course, as one chairman of a regulated utility engagingly told me, "if I can persuade the regulators that a block of concrete is in the rate base, I can earn my 12 per cent on it." I suspect that huge ground floor of a prime Manhattan office block, designated some years ago as a phone shop, fell into that category. In another wrinkle, when the United States gas industry found itself in 1969 with insufficient further reserves acquirable in the lower forty-eight states – that is from the traditional gas fields of Texas and its neighbours – it was in a quandary. The Federal Power Commission rules would not allow investment in pipeline capacity unless reserves could be proved to provide twenty years of flow at the capacity designated. The implications were unpleasant: no more reserves, no more capital expansion; no capital expansion, no increase in rate base – indeed a reduction, as the existing plant was depreciated in value. Reduction in rate base causes a reduction in the profits allowed – and the stock market does not like negative growth companies. Well, that quandary certainly set some intelligent minds working back in 1969. Much of the effort was directed in ways that could help solve the real public problem – the shortage of gas. Imaginative schemes to encourage wildcat drilling, and a frantic search for new sources, in Canada, the Gulf of Mexico, Alaska, and elsewhere. Some explored the techniques of producing gas from fossil fuels, in which Britain had made so much progress before the North Sea bonanza. A few, however, devoted their ingenuity to manipulating the system. I believe one interstate company, for example, altered its tariff structure, so as to encourage its wholesale customers to buy summer gas from an interstate competitor – making its own load more peaky, thus justifying a pipeline expansion on the same reserves!

The United States system certainly does not give much operating freedom to the monopolist. Each year, the regulators approve the capital expenditure that will be accepted in the rate base, and challenge the monopolist on the details of his operating expenditure.

But for all its potential for absurdity, and the detailed control year by year by regulators, and the near interminable legal proceedings, the American system does make sure that the monopolist serves the public. If sufficient individual consumers feel aggrieved, they have a clear way open through the political process to influence the regulatory body in their State, and to send the necessary signals to the utility in a form that cannot be ignored. When AT & T's Californian subsidiary irritated its regulators – for whatever cause – its circumstances became quite painful. Even though the return on capital formula was quite generous, by the time the regulator had disallowed capital expenditures and disallowed operating expenses, profits disappeared – and so did the bond rating. No board of directors can ignore that sort of message!

CONVINCING ECONOMICS – FOR THE MOMENT

In contrast, while the British system of regulation, built perhaps on theory, without the searing experience of America's nineteenth-century robber barons, is economically respectable, it does seem to encourage antisocial behaviour in the monopolist. The formula that regulates BT's prices for monopoly services (RPI − X%), has at least two virtues missing in the American system: it does not need detailed investigation more than once every seven years or so, and it encourages the monopolist to be economically efficient. The formula was derived from the novel method BT introduced in 1979 to buy electronic telephone exchanges. The new contract for TXE4 exchanges, placed with STC in that year, stated fixed prices falling each year along a path of assumed efficiency improvement. If the manufacturer could do better, he could keep the difference. Unfortunately, the formula has two flaws in regulating a utility; it only works well in a booming economy, and it protects the monopolist from public pressure for years at a time. So far so good, as the man said falling past the fifteenth floor. So far, a strong economy and the limited market share taken by the one permitted competitor, have given BT ideal circumstances for achieving real reductions in unit costs. Happily, in telecommunications the marginal cost of carrying additional traffic is relatively low, with all the new technologies in transmission and in multiplexing messages. So, RPI − 4.5 per cent has been handsomely achieved in boom conditions; but what if there should be a slump? Well, that is perhaps an issue for another day, but the day will come!

More urgent is the inability of the monopoly customer to signal displeasure at poor service. Trivial payments for missed appointments and delayed repair are really not good enough. Experience in the United States has shown that a monopolist in full possession of his powers needs a bigger voltage in the corrective electric shock. What analyst would notice £1 million in penalties when profits before tax are £2 billion? Perhaps the regulators for Telecom, Gas, Electricity, and so on should launch each year class actions on behalf of all monopoly customers, to fix damages for poor service. Of course fair standards would have to be set, and due allowance made for *force majeure* such as strikes. But is this not the only way that RPI − X% can represent the workings of a competitive market place? In a true market, if a supplier damages the values of a customer, that customer has choice, and can take his business elsewhere. Sound regulation should provide a threat of similar magnitude to poor monopoly service as well.

NEMESIS

Value as perceived by the customer; that principle seems to offer safe guidance in every sort of productive effort. Certainly in the competitive market place, failure to offer such value brings its own penalties swiftly. When markets are turbulent, success comes to those who can judge their customer's values well, and meet those criteria fast and efficiently. Where the market is not so perfect, and customers are constrained in their choice, the principle is no less valid; it just takes a little longer for the penalties of failure to hit home.

PUBLIC WEALTH THROUGH PUBLIC SERVICE

Earlier in this book, we saw how a fire brigade transformed the quality of its service through considering how to bring greater value to its customers, even though it received no payment for that value. Its benefits came in honour and recognition for its leaders, resources for its service, and public approval – which must be worth something. Other aspects of public service offer similar opportunities for creating wealth, in the broader definition encouraged by John Stuart Mill.[9]

Take education, for example. The distinction between teaching and causing a student to learn can distinguish between the introverted dedication to professional standards and the desire to deliver value perceived by the customer. This is why the arrangements for monitoring Britain's national curriculum can bring such benefits. With implementation starting in 1990, the progress of each student will be measured at the ages of seven, eleven, fourteen, and sixteen across a wide range of attainment targets defined in the subjects specified in the curriculum. With English, mathematics and science in the core curriculum, every young person of sixteen should have at least some of the basic intellectual equipment needed for life in the twenty-first century.

Strangely, when this approach was first mooted, the traditional fallacies of introverted professionalism were paraded: "If we teach well and the child doesn't learn, it has a learning problem"! Not the smallest benefit of the new approach lies in the reversal of that observation: "If the child doesn't learn, it is because you – the teacher – have a teaching problem." Success in the new frame of values will surely bring deeper satisfaction to all concerned. When the child learns, wealth – in the broadest sense – is surely created. Assessing how much has been learnt across the whole range of criteria at regular intervals, should make certain that unfruitful teaching methods do not destroy the ability of future teachers to create value in their turn. What the best educators have long known will become the norm for all; the respect of students, and admiration for the profession. Wealth creation brings benefit to all.

How do we measure?

Here, though, government is in danger of spoiling a good concept by an unhelpful emphasis. The greatest harvest from measuring a child's capability against a standard, lies surely in finding out where help is needed; the performance of the teacher or the school can no doubt be measured too – but not without damaging the diagnosis, if Goodhart's Law applies in education as it does in the banking system. Professor Charles Goodhart, of the London School of Economics, observed that any measure used with weight to regulate the banking system becomes debased as loopholes are found. Look at the fate of M3, the favourite money supply measure in the early 1980s, determining how fast banks, and therefore the economy, could expand – manipulated, useless, and now abandoned. We do not want that to happen to diagnostic assessment of a child's learning, I take it.

Health too is an industry often in the public service, but very closely concerned with value as perceived by the customer. Certainly in Britain, the National Health Service, with its one million employees, and £25 billion a year of expenditure, is a massive industry affecting virtually every individual. "Doctor knows best" can be justified, where it brings peace of mind to the patient; the principle, though, when joined with administration on such a massive scale, is a powerful formula for introversion. What is truly in the patient's interests may be hard to establish, but must be worth seeking.

In providing care for the frail elderly, the introverted professional approach can give solutions far from the real interests of old people themselves. To a dedicated hospital administrator, concerned with wards, beds, budgets, nurses, and waiting lists, the affair can seem straightforward, if impossible. "Just give me another £5 million a year, and we'll provide a geriatric bed for every frail old person in this town!" But perhaps that is not what they really want; after all, even the best geriatric ward is less agreeable than a family home. Perhaps a health manager truly concerned with delivering value as perceived by the client, should try to see that most old people do not end up in a hospital ward at all. That will certainly need initiatives outside the hospital, hard for an introvert to contemplate.

What has to happen? Perhaps one should start by understanding why so many old people today are rejected by their families, and fall on the public service as a last resort. If we assume no general reduction in filial affection in modern times, we must still contemplate the pressures on families living stressed working lives in cramped accommodation. Then an incontinent and querulous old person can be a trigger for immoderate irritation. So perhaps the enlightened health manager should focus on that objective: making it easier for families to look after their elderly relatives at home. In my experience, there is a series of measures, each of which costs a fraction of a nursed geriatric bed, and each capable of offering true value to an old person – domestic life in domestic surroundings. Incontinence aids, free laundry service, volunteer visitors and companions, day centres, and, perhaps most valuable of all, respite beds so that the family can take a holiday, sure that the old aunt will be soundly cared for. Some of those measures can be provided from within a hospital; others need support from the community. However, a public health service that can encourage the whole range of support to appear, can surely be said to create wealth. Certainly, the sum of human happiness will be increased.

FALLACIES IN FEED BACK

While in the fire service, education, and health – and no doubt in many other public services – wealth can be created even though it may not be easily measured, the greatest difficulties for judgement lie in those services which appear to be commercial while at least in part providing value not recognised in the cash transaction. In public transport, for example, there is superficially every appearance of a straightforward commercial organisation trading for profit. And yet, in a crowded city, a public subway or bus service is a near monopoly, and customers are not able to reflect in their trading pattern any loss of value through delay, crowding, dirt, or danger. In London or Manhattan, great international financial centres depend upon the efficient working of the public transport system, with no effective means of signalling any loss in their ability to create wealth caused by deficiencies in those systems.

Paradoxically, it seems easier for a non-trading monopoly service – like the fire brigade – to arrive at the whole economic value of a new initiative. The West Midlands Fire Service was able to do that in justifying its new computer system. In the British telecommunications system, however, there was during the 1970s a strange fallacy in the processes of economic evaluation that had unfortunate consequences. Understandably enthused with the merits of evaluating capital projects according to their Net Present Value, a single stipulation limited the quality of new British tele-communications equipment for several years. The stipulation? "In calculating net present value, you may not count any benefit for which the corporation does not receive payment or save cost." Where that criterion was rigorously applied, for example in the design of TXE4 exchanges during the early 1970s, the pressure was clearly to eliminate features that brought improved value for the customer, unless costs of maintenance could be reduced. After all, a monopoly customer of an essential service will buy whether the quality is good or no! Fortunately, in that same great business, principles carried over from an earlier and less narrow concept of public service persisted in many crucial areas. So the great International Gateway Exchange, at Mondial House on the bank of the Thames, was provided with diesel generating power capable of lighting a city – in case power failures should threaten the inter-national telephone service. Similarly, submarine cables were built to parts of the world that would have been cheaper served by satellite – because quality of transmission would be better and circuits more swift to repair. Whether such policies can survive the rigours of RPI − X% in a slump, will be worth watching. I doubt it.

WEALTH CREATORS ALL

So, seeking to create wealth by improving value as perceived by the customer – whoever that might be – seems a prescription valuable throughout an economy and a society. It can instil sound principles into government bureaucracies. Public servants, so often introverted and therefore bureaucrats concerned with procedure, will turn outwards and perhaps – who knows – become agile and flexible in serving the public. The trading monopolies will recognise that their power to damage or to enhance the value of their customers goes far beyond the simple trading transaction itself, and will consider the whole value to the public that they are capable of generating. And finally, those competing in turbulent markets will learn better how to anticipate the needs of their customers, and to prevent the opposition. In public service and private trade alike, creating value as perceived by the customer is the one sure principle for prosperity. Pursue the significant, not the merely measurable.

NOTES

1 Jacques Gernet, *History of Chinese Civilisation*, tr. J. R. Foster (Cambridge University Press, Cambridge, 1982).
2 Witold Rodzinski, *The Walled Kingdom* (Fontana, London, 1988), p. 121.
3 Humphrey Trevelyan, *The India we Left* (Macmillan, London, 1972), p. 56.
4 Pliny, *Epistolarum: Liber X*, ed. Ascensius (Roigny, Paris, 1533), p. 130.
5 Edward Gibbon, *The History of the Decline and Fall of the Roman Empire* (Strahan and Cadell, London, 1776–1788).
6 Charles Diehl, *Cambridge Medieval History*, vol. IV, ed. J. R. Tanner, C. W. Previté-Orton and Z. N. Brooke (Cambridge University Press, Cambridge, 1923), p. 762.
7 Edith Sitwell, *Alexander Pope* (Faber & Faber, London, 1930), p. 266.
8 K. N. Chaudhuri, *Trade and Civilisation in the Indian Ocean* (Cambridge University Press, Cambridge, 1986), p. 60.
9 John Stuart Mill, *Principles of Political Economy* (Parker, London, 1848).

PART IV

ARIA or MADRIGAL?

PARADOXES abound: liberate the individual, but harness the creative spirit; be venturesome, yet prudent; delegate, don't abdicate; achieve now, yet preserve the future. How can they be reconciled?

Who will prosper? What attitudes, aspects and aspirations promote; what fallacies and foibles destroy? History can teach, and new men win with proven style. Principles of leadership can translate, when they are drawn from turbulence and relate to the springs of human response. Impresarios bring out human talent.

Whole personalities are the men and women for the new age; the crabbed introvert constrains. Have fun!

7

THE INDIVIDUAL AND THE CORPORATION

FREEDOM WITHIN THE LAW

THE actors move sedately along the bridgeway, carried forward through the centuries from some fifteenth-century Shogun's palace. Past the third, second, and first pine,[1] the players in a *Nōh* drama move to the naming place at the back left-hand corner of the stage, or to the gazing pillar on the front left. Music comes from the flute pillar, and the *waki* makes his comments from the appointed place. The conventions of the *Nōh* play certainly create a structure. A structure that provides a framework for the most delicate nuances of meaning, as slight variations in tone or position show up strongly against the immutable framework. That particular convention, initiated in the fourteenth century and confirmed in its form 300 years later, has made possible sensitive analyses of a great variety of human relationships. But whether concerned with fishergirls in Suma bay, or the love affair between Prince Genji and Miyasu-dokoro, a *Nōh* play represents just a tiny part of the human condition; *King Lear* or even *The School for Scandal* could not have been contained within its limits.

For the individual, structure is crucial for the creative process, let alone the harnessing of many efforts towards a common goal. But that structure must be capable of development. For all the romantic associations of the nineteenth-century anarchists – Prince Kropotkin and others – their creed is essentially sterile; freedom that leaves the individual in an amorphous soup stunts the facility to create. For that, structure is needed. For those concerned to nurture a fruitful relationship between the individual and the organisation, the art of creating structures is subtle, and immensely important for success.

Like the three faces in the advertisements for Erasmic shaving sticks forty years ago, not too little, not too much, but just right!

The Japanese are renowned for their structured approach to commerce; structure based on the widest consultation is seen to bring a commitment and convergence in world markets quite awesome, as industry after industry in the West staggers from the blows. Should others copy them? They used a similar style in war; would it perhaps be fruitful to examine the consequences then, and consider whether theirs is an approach for all seasons? Field Marshal Slim, in *Defeat into Victory*, gives some pungent observations on the Japanese leadership style in Burma:[2]

The Japanese, in the earlier stages of the campaign, gained the moral ascendancy over us that they did, because we never seriously challenged their seizure of the initiative. They bought that initiative, fairly and inevitably, by paying for it with preparation ... The Japanese were ruthless and bold as ants while their designs went well, but if those plans were disturbed or thrown out – ant-like again – they fell into confusion, were slow to readjust themselves, and invariably clung too long to their original schemes ...

and, in a training message to his troops, in 1943:[3]

If the Japanese are allowed to hold the initiative they are formidable. When we have it, they are confused and easy to kill. By mobility away from roads, surprise, and offensive action we must regain and keep the initiative.

On that evidence, supported too by American experience throughout the bypassing campaigns of Admiral Nimitz and General MacArthur in the West Pacific, it seems that such deliberate and rigid leadership is a privilege for the guy on top – while he stays there! It took the Japanese commander on Bougainville, for example, four months to respond to an unexpected landing by Admiral Halsey's marines, with a garrison of 60,000, three to one superior in numbers. The counter-attack, when it came, was brave, but wiped out.

Flexible structures, then, that is what we need in turbulence; but is it? If the structure is very flexible in all its parts, is it not approaching anarchy? People do need givens if they are to turn outwards; for sure, in a very large organisation, the chief executive needs to beware how frequently the signals are changed. It may take more than a year for a significant alteration in the structure, strategy, or values to be understood everywhere in a group with several layers, even with imaginative use of modern communications. Any further change within that period can only confuse, as contrasting themes meet and compete in the heart of the organisation.

Even where confusion is avoided, changing basic principles of behaviour can be quite damaging to the creative process, as the instinct for self-preservation and readjustment to the prevailing wind absorbs energy. "Every time you reorganise, you bleed", one senior manager wrote after yet another reorganisation of Britain's rail system in the 1960s; just like a surgical operation, perhaps vital for future health, but first post-operative shock. As we can so often see, all but the most confident fear the worst for themselves during periods of uncertainty, turning their minds inwards to self-protection in the combats within the organisation, absorbing energy more profitably turned outwards to the customer and his values.

LICENCE AND LIBERTY

What is the healthy balance between established certainties and regeneration, in the framework for individuals? Some characteristics of structure should perhaps be seen as permanent in most organisations; long-term objectives, and the construct of values that determine how individuals approach the great variety of issues that come unexpectedly over the horizon.

Privatisation of public utility monopolies has shown the damage that can flow from a careless denigration of established values. Notions held by former public servants, of the prevailing ethics in private ownership and competition, can be wide of the mark; many may believe that, once privatised, ruthless self-interest should be the norm. The ideals of public service, however imperfectly followed, may be rather more agreeable for the customer.

Changing the balance between care for customer safety on the one hand, and short-term cost reduction on the other may well have contributed to the ill-fame of London's underground system, for example. As in so many situations, the pressure on individuals to achieve short-term financial results turns attention away from the longer term, the unlikely and the hard to measure. The enquiry into the catastrophic fire at King's Cross rail station heard hours of evidence on rubbish accumulating out of sight under escalators, of staff ignorant of the simplest safety measures and even where fire extinguishers could be found. Paint seems to have been chosen for ease in cleaning graffiti, even though fire made it produce clouds of toxic gas. That sad, well-documented pattern of blinkered management action, so possible when values change haphazardly under ill-considered pressures, could be matched many times over, in other industries and where catastrophes are less public.

WIN, AND SURVIVE

Competitive individuals playing contact sports to win, need clear rules and firm refereeing. AT & T, which before its enforced dismemberment was renowned throughout the world for the quality of its telecom services, seemed to me to have had a rather sound balance in place. Individuals were indeed required to achieve excellent financial results, but only after they had taken care of standards in quality of service that were not for debate; it was just no good arguing that a little shading in the repair service would make a higher financial return possible; but even they had problems in California. In a monopoly, individuals who are under short-term pressures for profit cannot be relied upon to resist short-term cuts in service, where those help to save money, unless the rules of the game quite clearly forbid them, or impose financial penalties that make the chiselling fruitless. "Don't even think of it," as my son tells the cat eyeing a piece of smoked salmon on the dining table. The message needs to be clear and retribution swift; after all, by the time complaints have worked up into a local fury, those excellent short-term results may have earned promotion for the individual responsible, leaving his successor to deal with the backlash!

Protecting longer-term interests is prudent in organisations of every kind, but perhaps most of all in the financial sector. The collapse of that great Chicago bank Continental Illinois carried potent lessons. In that structure, individuals competing for promotion to the highest ranks saw that their immediate personal objectives would be best served by producing startling short-term results. In lending money, bankers have a very clear temptation; borrowers with risky projects, or borrowers with no intention to repay, are usually tolerant of rather high interest rates. While it can be prudent to lend for high risk projects, the analyses must be thorough and knowledgeable, the criteria for repayment related to the achievement of forecasts, and a reasonable relationship established between enhanced risk and the higher rate of interest. After all, if a certain class of lending implies a 1 per cent risk of bad debts each year, that might be acceptable if the interest charges were 2 per cent higher or more; that higher risk would be covered by the higher return. Tricky, though, if a whole class of borrower is overextended and falls on hard times. Tempting too to be optimistic, when the short-term profit for each dollar lent looks so good. Nemesis caught up with those Continental executives and their organisation when the value of oil leases crashed, jeopardizing the bank as a whole. On other occasions, a merchant bank, Morgan Grenfell, was so keen to win for its client, Guinness, that it damaged its reputation through overly tough tactics. Bank executives in the United States were tempted to illegal trading to improve corporate results; others just did it for money!

How should one manage the paradox? On the one hand, the need for individual executives to act aggressively in building business; on the other, the danger that such individuals may sacrifice prudence and longer-term interests in order to shine brightly when bonuses and promotions are imminent. One British bank sticks to a practice discarded as hopelessly old-fashioned by the tigers. In Singer and Friedlander, all the directors in a division of the bank sit in the same large room – corporate finance, investment management, and so on. That way, as the great banking partnerships have discovered over the centuries, the actions of each individual are transparent to the others. The benefits clearly lie in early warning of headstrong or selfish behaviour; but even more valuable is the mutual support that can make each individual more effective. Again, in that bank the leading people are rewarded by a share in the profits of the whole; the size of the slice determined by the personal contribution made over time. In other institutions, huge instant payments related to personal performance seem to carry dangers for the corporation all the more serious as the pressures on the individual become more intense. Control is all the more difficult when the sinners so often part in a golden parachute!

A spate of catastrophes in recent years has shown how dangerous unsound value systems can be in other industries too. One danger comes when an organisation is capable of having an effect on the community far beyond the simple transactions with which it is directly concerned. The catastrophe of Aberfan in 1966 is one example. In the enquiry as to how colliery managers allowed a huge unstable mountain of spoil to accumulate above a Welsh village occupied by their own miners, one point came out clearly. Mine managers believed that their concerns were with coal, underground.[4] Rock and earth piled high outside the mine was not their affair – or seemed not to be, although many of them lived in the community that was threatened. Similarly, public transport managers who believe that their first priorities lie in running trains safely, may neglect the safety of their passengers once they have left the tracks for the station and the street.

Managers of telecommunication services seem often quite unaware of the extent of damage that poor service can create for their customers – because for so many there is no effective way of signalling that economic damage in a way that relates to the values inculcated in the monopolist. What a fallacy, to give a benefit zero value just because you are not able to measure it accurately. Quite a common fallacy indeed, in the old world of certainties. It was not such a big leap from the old engineers' adage "if you cannot measure it, you do not know much about it", to assuming that if you cannot measure it, it does not exist! A phrase of the Archbishop of York in 1988, "has it occurred to you that lust for certainty may be a sin", may have economic as well as spiritual significance.

LET THE SUN IN!

In the new turbulent age, sound value systems are those that encourage the individual to look outwards; to look from the self-regarding certainties of the administrator, out towards those who use our products and services or relate to us in their own working lives. This outward aspect of the individual is not just for those who work outside corporate buildings, meeting the world. Rather as in pruning a rose bush, the buds spring where the sun reaches the wood. So, an outwardly turned attitude of mind is fruitful deep in the heart of a corporate structure.

Geoff Mulcahy has given some tales of introverted attitudes he found in the British Woolworths, while it was hunkered down, under siege with falling sales and poor profits. Facility managers were proud to save money through turning down the lights; that customers found it difficult to see the goods on sale seemed less important to them. Enthusiasm was reserved for cutting stock shrinkage, as the euphemism has it, and sales staff preferred the friendly comfort of the stockroom to the turmoil of the counter. Distribution patterns minimised transport costs, while letting stores run out of goods. As he explained, in transforming the business, facing outwards implies also treating each colleague as a customer, seeking to create value as he or she judges it.

Rank Xerox went through the same process in their Total Quality programme. Defining quality as the characteristics that the customer needs – no more, no less – some departments were quite disconcerted to discover that much of what they did for introverted reasons was not at all helpful to the unfortunate recipients; indeed, one information section learned that most of its reports were regarded as useless, fit only for door stops and props for screens, once its people took the trouble to ask their internal customers if they were getting value in their terms. Those self-regarding values, so prevalent in the old functional hierarchies, where a colleague across the boundary was not of one's own specialism, and therefore could have no valid view on the quality of one's work, are just incompatible with the fast-moving markets of today, where customers are used to choosing from a rich variety of eager competitors. They are incompatible too in the public service and in monopolies, because although their customers are trapped in one relationship, they have learned to look for something more than the ration book and the bureaucratic brush-off in the rest of their needs.

ARE MONOPOLISTS HAPPY?

Even though most businessmen try to achieve more market share, and monopoly is no doubt seen as the ultimate attainment in that laudable pursuit, monopolies bring almost as much danger to their own as to the rest of us. Few are loved by those beyond their protective walls. Peter Gibbings, formerly chairman of the *Guardian*, has the pretty metaphor of monopoly looking like a new-born babe – "Hideous to everyone except its proud possessor" – and that little paradox gave the public relations profession quite a lot of trade in the bad old days of Organisation Man.

But the internal demerits of monopoly are legion too: introversion, bureaucracy, delay, and the siege mentality. As we put it to Telecom staff in 1979: "Think of the monopoly not as a defensive wall, but as a barrier to your true potential." In seeking to resist technology, relying on the strength of monopoly to preserve obsolete jobs, they would merely forfeit new opportunities; and the force of public pressure had to break through in the end. In a military analogy, the danger in retreating behind fixed fortifications is taught to every officer. The siege mentality can cripple initiative, and leave the defenders ignorant of what the outside world is up to, and what it plans. The fighting patrol, probing the enemy's position beyond the defensive barrier, helps morale as much as it provides information. Every leader of a monopoly needs some competitive businesses at least, and would do well to pass high fliers through that stimulating experience once or twice, to tone up the sensitivities.

WHO ARE THESE PEOPLE?

If embedding good quality throughout an organisation makes understanding what other people value rather important, and how they think, there does seem to be a need for people to share personal cultures, or at least to be able to assess those around them. In Britain, where perhaps there tends to be a rather more pronounced social exclusivity than elsewhere, sharing culture can require quite an effort. Whether in education, taste, accent, dress, or profession, British people still seek to flock with their like. It has been a problem for years, illustrated 150 years ago by Benjamin Disraeli in *Sybil*, and in Gustave Doré's illustrations of London half a century later. Then the distinction was primarily between the rich and the poor; between gentlemen and trade. Now, the divisions are more complex, but similarly marked by an introverted concern for group values – a powerful inhibition in transferring ideas. Evelyn Waugh, visiting his parents in north London, found some architect neighbours in the room; "Who are these dreadful people?" was the phrase treasured by them. Wilfred Thesiger, an exemplary gentleman, met him in Addis Ababa, at the coronation of Haile Selassie; his comment?[5]

I disapproved of his grey suede shoes, his floppy bow tie and the excessive width of his trousers: he struck me as flaccid and petulant and I disliked him on sight. Later he asked me, at second hand, if he could accompany me into the Danakil country, where I planned to travel. I refused. Had he come, I suspect only one of us would have returned.

And they both came from Oxford!

What yawning differences in culture exist everywhere, between, for example, the technologists in a commercial organisation and those responsible for leading business units. What gaps between suppliers and customers, government and industry, academia and the trading world, and finally, with the greatest significance for economic growth, between the financiers and the entrepreneurs who need their money to add value and to build. Only the Japanese seem consistently to bridge the gaps.

DIALOGUES OF THE DEAF

Every organisation, indeed, experiences the dialogue of the deaf, between those who understand information technology, for example, and those other individuals who are capable of improving a public service or winning a competitive battle but fear the new mystery. And yet neither the organisation can prosper, nor the information technology professionals get their funds, unless that gap is bridged. Hence, no doubt, the prosperity of those few consultants who can speak with equal confidence in the boardroom and with the acolytes who serve the computers in hushed tones.

Not that it is so difficult, as BT and some other organisations have shown, to find a common language in which both scientists and businessmen can meet with a common mind. If the scientist can reduce the complexity of his options to a simple statement of technical objective and the resources required to achieve it, then the scientist and the businessman are on common ground. On the one hand, "I can reasonably expect to give you X in eighteen months at a cost of £500,000", and on the other, "If I had X, I could expect to generate a return of Y per cent on what the scientists tell me the development will cost." Of course the scientist will need to express his uncertainties in probabilities, but the businessman has his imponderables too. The key surely is for each to form a view derived from the factors that he can understand, expressed in terms that are of value to the other. The benefit to the scientist in having his project evaluated as an un-mysterious investment capable of generating wealth is obvious. He can break out from the constrained atmosphere of a controlled overhead into the rich pasture of the productive wealth creators!

How much smoother the whole process of transferring technology seems when a scientific culture pervades an organisation! Take Celltech, notably successful in bio-engineering and in the more managerial skills of getting approval for clinical trials and the sale of pharmaceuticals for humans. There a project manager is named right at the start of a new product, who takes responsibility through to market launch. That way, one person, well below the chief executive, is inspired to judge rigorously at the start the hopeful estimates of the project champion. Once committed, an incentive to use the ingenuity in chasing success that can only come when one is proving one's own judgement! The project manager prowls through the system cajoling help where it can best be found; "there is always something else an able person would rather do, if your project looks boring," says one of them. Only a last and unsatisfactory resort, to ask a director to make an order, "you must make people want to help you". So much easier if they care about the same things as you do.

That too, however, can have its dangers, when three-quarters of the cost of launching a new product lie in the pivotal studies to satisfy the regulators; the cost of travelling hopefully with a product that eventually proves to be toxic can damage the ability of a small company to take a better idea through to success. So that fundamental characteristic of the scientific mind – the willingness to destroy a beautiful hypothesis with an ugly fact, as T. H. Huxley put it[6] – becomes plain commercial good sense. Tricky to get the right balance, though, between defeatism and blind optimism; perhaps that is one boon that a science education for all could bring us. Would the glorious disaster of Arnhem have happened, had Generals Montgomery and Browning learned the way sound scientists think? Surely that late discovery of two Panzer divisions among nearby trees would have shelved their beguiling plan to leap forward a bridge too far. Professor John Carroll of Cambridge University once described to me how he saw the mechanism for scientific progress: "As an academic, I am under intense pressure to publish; but once my paper is public, my closest colleague would feel a duty to tear it apart." Sounds alarming, but a stimulating process for opening up new lines of advance, and for abandoning the blind alleys after the first few steps. Not a bad philosophy for the entrepreneur perhaps, or the chief executive trying to get some fruitful creativity out of the *apparatchiks*.

If it is difficult to bridge culture within a company, it is even more so between those who supply technology and the customer who receives it. Most obvious in very large organisations, where purchasing officers often have power but limited understanding, either of the technology on offer or of the business use in which that technology could generate wealth. The problem is compounded when innovators in small firms are still further separated from users, by large intermediaries controlling the commercial relationship. Hence the welcome given in the United States to Secretary Weinberger's Small Business Innovation Research Program in 1982. Though still spending only $450 million by 1987, the signal was out that clever small teams could reach right through into the Department of Defense on their own feet. There is, of course, the understandable argument put forward by those who write procurement contracts for large purchasers, that small suppliers may have weak balance sheets insufficient to support the strains of a big order. Others too argue that the large intermediary can understand better the decision-making process in the large purchaser, and then guide the small innovator with the benefit of other experience. However strong these two arguments may be, the transfer of technology is inhibited if capable innovators are separated by organisational and commercial layers from direct contact with those who need the solutions in order to win, whether in the market place or on the battlefield. That has been especially crippling in Eastern Europe, wherever the Foreign Trade Corporation or its equivalent insists on handling all contacts outside the country.

PURCHASING FALLACIES

If those complexities of trading structure are further exacerbated by traditional purchasing policies in which price is directly related to cost, the flow of good technology is further impaired. In the development of System X, for example, the second generation of the processor showed an improvement in power per pound of cost by nearly two orders of magnitude – one hundred-fold. Is it surprising that its vigorous exploitation had to wait for the introduction of true competition, and the final expulsion of cost-plus profit calculations from the scene? Earlier, the Monarch PABX saw manufacturing costs halved in little more than a year, under the stimulus of direct competition, and now sells in more than forty countries. If a monopsony/monopoly relationship is inevitable, then the $RPI - X\%$ approach, first introduced in the purchasing of TXE4 exchanges at the end of the 1970s, has at least the merit of giving the supplier an economic incentive to introduce low cost technology faster; outright competition adds the additional threat of losing market share!

WHAT IS AN ASSET

Perhaps if non-scientific managers find it difficult to value the products of their own laboratories, we should not be surprised that the managers of pension funds and the other institutions that dominate our financial markets, should so often give up the task at the first attempt. It is of course said that if a company has consistently shown its ability in the past to turn research and development investment to future wealth, it will earn the financiers' proper valuation for such investment today. While the argument has perhaps some merit − it is certainly frequently used − it falls down if the company concerned is growing rapidly, is changing direction, or is in the throes of a major transformation in technology. The problem of non-communicating cultures is certainly made worse by the huge concentration of ownership power in the hands of such funds − due, as Philip Chappell points out, to an unhealthy bias in the tax treatment of personal savings, in Britain and in other countries too. When the power to invest moves, under the influence of skewed tax rates, to huge insurance companies or investment trusts, a few Organisation Men can influence the development of whole industries. As Organisation Men are wont, they tend to follow fashion among their own kind, fearful to fall away from the index.

Perhaps a diversity of individual investors would be neither so short-term nor so introverted as the *apparatchiks* of the great financial institutions; each could develop a greater understanding for, and loyalty to, the particular companies in his personal portfolio. At present, a company that may need to invest 15 per cent of sales each year on research and development and on information and computing systems, to catch up with its competitors or to steal a march, may meet an unsympathetic hearing from its stockholders.

To move easily among the cultures, our present-day renaissance individual need not aspire to match Leonardo Da Vinci's universal creativeness, but he or she does need the training, attitude of mind, and outward aspect that can alone bridge these gaps in understanding, so dangerous in turbulence. When Organisation Man prospered, with markets and technologies evolving predictably, the autocrats with their staffs could design the procedures for moving knowledge about within the organisation, defining each person's role; in rapid change, that process has to spark among individuals, responding to the opportunities of the moment. Professor Gene Rochlin's illumination of how a US aircraft carrier works in action[7] shows that happening in a surprising way. The admiral may direct the movements of the task force, but the safe arrival and flight of aircraft at the frequency of O'Hare on a pitching deck comes from the co-ordinated actions of hundreds of enlisted men, reacting on informal networks, fast.

Is it smart to be macho?

If the modern organisation depends so crucially on the spontaneous relationships among individuals, the interaction of the sexes offers fresh possibilities when sympathy and understanding become necessary aspects of every individual's personal behaviour. Fortunately, women in modern organisations are resisting Professor Higgins's plea to become more like men! Well, perhaps some masculine characteristics help – if one can safely generalise. A certain amount of aggression can be valuable at the right moment, and the bulldog qualities of tenacity and resilience have their place too, since large organisations – like super-tankers – can be a long time in the turning. However, in a world where sympathy with the other person's point of view and a disposition to mould oneself malleably to the dictates of events are becoming so important, perhaps we should encourage men to develop some characteristics that have usually been regarded as feminine. Sadly, many women still find it easier to become managers in functions that are often inward looking and procedural – personnel and purchasing, for example.

Strange, when in world history the most extraordinary progress has been made while women rule, that so few have yet broken through into general management in industry and commerce. With Queen Elizabeth as a sixteenth-century heroine, and Queen Anne presiding over the extraordinary victories of Marlborough, women have proved rather successful as chief executives at the national level, or, as Queen Victoria's prosperous reign confirmed in the nineteenth century, as a patron above the fray. Maria Theresa was a noble and successful Queen of Hungary and Bohemia, and Archduchess of Austria, while bearing five sons and eleven daughters; she even achieved immortality throughout the male worlds of Arabia and North Africa in the Maria Theresa dollar that was common currency with the gold sovereign, until the greenback took over. Russia's two Catherines were as powerful as any Tsar, and no worse rulers.

India and Britain have found strong women leaders. Why have these historical figures succeeded so well? Partly, perhaps, because of that intuition, but also surely – in most cases – due to a skill in handling people that encourages initiative, without seeking to steal the glory. "I consider you and your officers as persons born for the preservation of your country", were words that must have moved the English admiral after the Armada victory. Mind you, Elizabeth had the aggressive talents too, saying one year earlier to the French ambassador:

The King of Spain is daily making offers of peace and friendship, but I shall not listen to them, knowing his ambition; On the contrary, I have sent Drake to ravage his coasts and am considering sending the Earl of Leycester to Holland to show that I am not afraid of war.

Certainly, deep in the feudal period, it must have been the chatelaines who ran the estates, while their pugnacious menfolk were away doing the chivalrous thing, as Steve Shirley suggests. Steve built a successful software company on the consequent principle, that many talented women at home have a capacity for business thinking that could be tapped through advanced technology, because tele-communications makes distance of little account.

FEEL, FOR A CHANGE!

While cartels and protective agreements made mechanical direction of organisations feasible, cold fish armed with their ratios and financial reports could pass for leaders. As one modern leader points out, if a general lost 100,000 men in 1915, his concern seemed first to be in finding replacements, rather than a new strategy. The static nature of that war in Flanders, and the rigid disciplined structure of command, forced those men to fight fruitless battles in great personal danger. In the mobile, turbulent and unexpected world of today, each individual needs to generate his own stimulus, the fire to find and drive forward his own solutions. For that, commitment is crucial, and emotion may not come amiss. Field Marshal Montgomery wrote, "the beginning of leadership is a battle for the hearts and minds of men" and "if the approach to this human problem is cold and impersonal, little can be achieved."[8]

What, emotion intruding in the cold logic of civilian affairs? Yes, I believe so. Certainly in one experience, facing sixty general managers in BT primed in caucus to demand restoration of differentials in personal pay, an emotional appeal to duty turned the edge. My OCTU speech, they called it, half in jest, but recalling that first lesson for the young officer, "look after your men before yourself". That foundation principle had been overwhelmed, even among senior managers, in the selfishness of rampant union power and the contempt for authority that the era of Organisation Man brought on itself. Self-interest is part of the human condition, but experience shows that a certain degree of disinterested concern for people on whom one depends makes good sense, even if it arises from logic rather than instinct. At any rate, that speech marked a turning point in the style of leadership throughout that huge corporation, even though I feared at first that it would sound corny to the cynics. It launched the first stage in facing outwards.

SIGNALLING SYSTEMS

There is more to motivation than money; that seems clear when so many of the greatest feats of courage and endurance – and creativity – have come from those who have gained little thereby in financial terms. Money, though, can provide a wonderfully sensitive signalling system. IBM's Individual Performance Review system, lifted painlessly into Britain's National Health Service, shows one effective way. Pay increases are linked to performance, assessed on a scale of five points. Even though for most health managers the distinction of a grade affects pay by only a few percentage points, that seems enough to carry home the message. Since for each individual, the assessment is based on achievement of tasks agreed with the next two higher levels of management, the connection is proving its value as an accurate means for focusing effort on essentials, even though the command structure itself is so confusingly complicated. With a district general manager reporting both to his own local authority and its chairman, and to the regional general manager next higher in the permanent structure, it is hard to conceive a better way to resolve misconceptions.

However, where material incentives are more powerful, and less carefully judged, they can cause great damage. When strong personal incentives in pay and promotion are attached to criteria that conceal catastrophe, the whole organisation may be imperilled, as we have seen in more than one banking scandal in London and New York. But while a single bonus scheme tied to group profits has its merits, fostering collegiate behaviour, it has its drawbacks too. In the Kingfisher Group, for example, four retailing businesses – B & Q, Comet, Superdrug, and Woolworth Stores – each have quite different styles and customer patterns. In a more extreme example, it is hard to see what incentive rewards based on Unilever's group performance would have for individuals in very different operating companies, whose own results would be drowned in the consolidated figures. If the value of money as a motivator is primarily to carry signals, marking exceptional performance so as to encourage more of the same, my own preference lies in awards that are generous, but more closely linked to achievement of the individual as he contributes to the immediate team. Certainly every organisation needs such signals to show where the harvest lies; hard work is just not enough if the results do not come through. In Woolworth's flattest years, its new chief executive found the car park was full by 7.30 am!

RESPONSIBILITY, DELEGATION AND ABDICATION

Stress, deliberately applied as a management tool, is fortunately losing favour. With the signs of stress so rarely found among chief executives, perhaps its cause is not so much the pressure of events – or even the pressure for results – as the frustration of responsibility without the power to act, so often felt by the creative individual forced into the Organisation Man mould. Perhaps when both strategy and tactics could be defined from on high, the damage to the organisation from the behaviour of individuals under stress was not so severe, and so pressure could safely be applied relentlessly. After all, the allotted task was defined in the procedures, and a good administrator would be sure to spot any odd idiosyncrasies of someone cracking up or running wild. Now it is rather different; when initiative is needed from so many, it must be comforting to feel sure that the springs for action come from healthy, balanced, and informed minds. A successful smile test may be a good guide to effectiveness, and even the most successful companies can claim to be happy, without jeopardising their share price.

Delegation is not a simple art, as many sad tales remind us. While moving the authority to act outwards in the organisation, matching devolved responsibility, is the essence of sound delegation, there are subtle skills in stimulating the individual without losing control of developments. In my experience, the most dangerous temptation to the senior manager is to tell a newly enfranchised individual how to do the job. The traps can be beguiling; "What do you advise me to do?" can be a difficult plea to resist. Yet, if the response is clear and didactic, responsibility for achievement moves instantly back to the shoulders of the senior manager. Organisation Men can be rather skillful: first, the review of alternatives, offering genuine choice, but with preference hinted. My response: "Well, I rather like your third option"; then the trap snaps shut. "MDT, (Managing Director Telecoms, Organisation Men love initials), we will take your plan and do our best to make it work; you are aware of the difficulties, which are recorded in the minutes." Toughened in that school, I came to prefer the Socratic response. Ask questions. Make sure that the position has been soundly assessed, but hold back your own opinions. That way responsibility remains with the power to act, rather than that most unhealthy of all situations – authority devolved, without obligation for the consequences.

In our new renaissance, the relationships between the individual and the corporation are complex and varied; getting them right for the particular situation is one of the new leader's crucial tasks. One thing, though, is certain: the right pattern will not be the one you inherited!

NOTES

1 Donald Keene (ed.), *Twenty Plays of the Nōh Theatre* (Columbia University Press, New York, 1970).

2 Field Marshal W. J. Slim, *Defeat into Victory* (Papermac, London, 1986), p. 537.
3 Ibid., p. 143.
4 Barry Turner, *Man-made Disasters* (Wykeham, London, 1978), p. 58.
5 Wilfred Thesiger, *The Life of My Choice* (Collins, London, 1987), p. 92.
6 T. H. Huxley, *Collected Essays*, vol. VIII (Macmillan, London, 1908), p. 244.
7 Gene Rochlin, La Porte, Roberts, "The self-designing, high reliability organization: aircraft carrier flight operations at sea", *Naval War College Review*, Autumn, 1987.
8 Field Marshal B. L. Montgomery, *The Path to Leadership* (Putnam, New York, 1961), pp. 10, 18.

8

THE SURVIVORS

Cogs on their spindles

In the world of Organisation Man, personal prosperity depended on understanding one's allotted role, and learning how to perform it rather well, not questioning too adventurously the dictates of higher authority. Tacitus gives the idea, in a speech from a Roman knight, Marcus Terentius, to the Emperor Tiberius.[1] "Tibi summum rerum judicium dei dedere: nobis obsequii gloria relicta est." ("To you the Gods have given the supreme judgement in affairs: To us remains the glory of obedience.") Terentius had his tongue in his cheek, but fortunately autocrats can be blinded by apparent flattery!

As William Whyte reminded us,[2] in the heyday of authority in our era individuals were required to specialise, and then to narrow further until they specialised within their specialisms. While most organisations worked within their predictable environments, with the future evolving from a well-ordered past, it was possible to organise men's efforts in that way, and indeed perhaps useful progress was made, with each individual contributing his or her own special skills to the well-ordered corporate clockwork. Cogs, but then clocks need cogs.

Perhaps, though, it was never quite so well ordered. Tolstoy wittily illustrates the cock-up theory of history in his account of the battle of Borodino in *War and Peace*.[3] Hooting at the idea that the French failed to win that battle in their usual style because Napoleon had a cold in his head, he asserted the influence of many thousands on what actually occurred, even under the autocratic power of a renowned military genius.

It was not Napoleon who ordained the course of the battle, because none of his instructions were put into execution, and he knew nothing of what was passing before him. Therefore the manner in which these men slaughtered one another did not depend on Napoleon's will, but proceeded independently of him, from the wills of the hundreds of thousands of men who took part in the affair. It *only seemed* to Napoleon that all was due to his will. And therefore the question whether Napoleon had or had not a cold in his head is of no more interest to history than the cold of the lowest soldier of the commissariat.

A BAND OF BROTHERS

There are perhaps fruitful truths in that assessment of men working within an organisation. Maybe it was not so much what Napoleon did on the field of Borodino that influenced its outcome, but rather his impression on the minds of all those French soldiers during the preceding decade of his leadership; on the day, Napoleon contributed the negative, "I will not demolish my Guard".[4]

In the same era, Horatio Nelson gave only the simplest instructions to his captains, relying on the individual responses among his "band of brothers", as they faced particular opportunities. At the battle of the Nile, it was Captain Foley of the *Goliath* who saw that the shoal water between the anchored line of French ships and the shore was just deep enough to allow a British attack on the unprepared landward quarter. As the United States Admiral Mahan put it,[5] "It is in entire keeping with Nelson's well-known character, that, after discussing all likely positions and ascertaining that his captains understood his views, he should with perfect and generous confidence have left all the details of immediate action with them." His book, *The Influence of Sea Power upon the French Revolution and Empire* carried Nelson's leadership style to generations of Annapolis men, for emulation by Admiral Halsey and others in the Pacific a century and a half later.

Nevertheless, few Organisation Men had the privilege of serving under such a leader; for them, the sardonic words of Terentius would have seemed appropriate.

Loosening up

For most people formed to fit within the old hierarchies, the skills learned then and the style of working will seem neither adequate nor fruitful in the turbulent events that most of us now face. Those monolith organisations, with their cascaded echelons of specialists, might have seemed appropriate for the age of cartels and monopolies, but they just had to go when competition arrived and hastened the pace of change. Leaving decisions to committees staffed with carefully balanced representation from the functional baronies was just too slow a process for determining where the course lies for action, when action is needed fast.

"Better approximately right than precisely wrong", was the phrase used to justify inflation accounting in those mad years following OPEC's drive to raise the price of oil. In a fast-moving world, that seems a sound adage for all of us, but impractical when each participant in a decision has the power of veto, and few are able to see the wider picture. When technology, the market or a competitor is moving fast, the decision made with good judgement, in a day, on the best facts available, is likely to be more fruitful than the perfectly argued consensus of a committee arriving a year too late. So today, in organisations of every kind, the authority to make decisions is being moved out to individuals close to the crucial issues – and that means close to the customer, for almost all of us. Just like Captain Foley on 1 August 1798, those best able to judge at the point where opportunity arises must have the power to act.

Think for yourself!

It follows, therefore, that those myriads who now have to act spontaneously, need also to judge soundly. Those who can do so in the variety of circumstances, and in the brief moments that a turbulent world will allow, are the sure survivors. Two thousand years ago, Julius Caesar took care that his officers were trained to think for themselves, and that helped him through many a crisis. Overwhelmed by a sudden attack by the Nervii, for example, at the battle of the Sambre,[6] they acted on their own initiative – "propter propinquitatem et celeritatem hostium nihil iam Caesaris imperium expectabant, sed per se quae videbantur administrabant", "they did not wait for orders from Caesar, but because the enemy was upon them, acted each as he saw fit") – and won the crucial victory in north-east Gaul.

So, in our own contests, forming managers who can judge well, rather than the highly polished cogs of yesterday, seems a rather important task facing each of us – as individuals seeking to prosper, and as leaders building organisations relevant to our times. McKinsey have done that rather well for years. They train their consultants to approach complex issues with a relaxed mind, relying on a well-instilled logical process. With that confidence, they can be free of preconceptions, thinking from first principles, rather than looking for problems to suit safe methodologies and prepackaged solutions. A well-learnt drill: identify the primary issue; define that, and then set out the secondary questions whose resolution delivers the first. Now you know what you have to find out and demonstrate. Coming at confusion that way has the nice virtue of ignoring all those tempting givens that are not relevant, while concentrating on just those facts that are vital, however spongy they may be; case study buffs find it quite disconcerting at first. Once grasped, that facility to find order in a maelstrom of seemingly pertinent irrelevancies gives the confidence to absorb the texture of a situation without fear of mental paralysis. Two adages: from the Royal Engineers, "time spent in reconnaissance is seldom wasted"; and a personal one, "if you are not at first confused, it's because you haven't understood the complexity of the problem".

People without confidence in their intellectual tools fear to leave their prejudices, lest they have no structure to survive by. Even Dr Samuel Johnson knew he lacked the equipment to defend his religious beliefs, and resented any attempt to disturb them, while eager for conflict in other fields. Peter Abelard, 800 years ago, was so confident in his own intellectual equipment that he was prepared to disturb blind faith: "by doubting we are led to inquiry; and from inquiry, we perceive the truth." But St Bernard reacted as Johnson would have done, and drove Abelard from teaching. So, be wary in proclaiming your insights, lest your puzzles rouse a dozing bear!

WHERE DO THE GOOD IDEAS COME FROM?

So judgement alone is not enough; Nelson's captains also had the ability to see, in tiny circumstances, the opportunity for creative initiative. For a few today, it seems that a happy intuition shows the same results – cabbage patch dolls or *Cats*, perhaps. Lucky prodigies; for most of us, a creative act first requires hard work. "Cette période de travail conscient préliminaire qui précède toujours tout travail inconscient fructueux." That great nineteenth-century mathematician, Henri Poincaré, makes the point clearly in his *Science et Méthode*[7] – "That period of conscious effort that always precedes fruitful intuition." Earlier, Dugald Stewart wrote in his *Elements of the Philosophy of the Human Mind*,[8]

when a man possesses an habitual fertility of invention in any particular Art or Science and can rely, with confidence, on his inventive powers, whenever he is called upon to exert them; he must first have acquired, by previous habits of study, a command over those classes of his ideas, which are subservient to the particular effort that he wishes to make.

It seems quite clear: if we wish to be consistently creative, we must furnish our minds with the necessary understandings. Those who take the trouble to do so, will be the survivors when creativity is crucial. In Sir Joshua Reynold's words, "The mind is but a barren soil . . . unless it be continuously fertilized and enriched with foreign matter."[9] The bricks for *The Rime of the Ancient Mariner* came from other men's works.[10]

Understanding, then, we need, and rules for thought – rules that encourage creative ideas, not those petty constraints so prevalent in bureaucratic structures. Sir Joshua has this to say:[11]

What we now call Genius, begins . . . where known, vulgar, and trite rules have no longer any place. It must of necessity be, that even the works of Genius, . . . as it must have its cause, must likewise have its rules; it cannot be by chance, that excellencies are produced with any constancy, or any certainty, for this is not the nature of chance.

Those leaders who can articulate these patterns for thought with just the right balance between the structure and opportunity, will help their colleagues prosper.

What are those rules going to be in the world of affairs? What should they cover, and what do they mean for the individual? They affect our attitudes, our aspect, the skills we need, and the way we behave with other people.

SYMPATHY PAYS

In our attitude, the prime need is to move away from that defensive retirement within our particular specialism, so characteristic of Organisation Man, towards an open co-operation in achievement. Prince Peter Kropotkin, reacting against Tsarist feudalism, saw in the anarchist "outgoing relationships . . . large natures, overflowing with tenderness, with intelligence, and with goodwill, and using their feeling, their intellect, their active force in the service of the human race without asking anything in return". Perhaps that benevolence, as Alan Ritter names it in *Anarchism*,[12] has its place in the practical world of affairs too, albeit within a more defined framework than a nineteenth-century revolutionary would willingly accept! In our aspect, then, we need to turn from those happy certainties in our own group judgements, towards a sympathetic understanding of other people's values. That is not just good citizenship; it is practical business sense. A customer with rich choice will turn to those who seem best to understand what really matters to him.

Sometimes quite simple people find it easier to enter into the situations of others than do highly trained professionals. Peter Anderson, long a farmer in Africa, tells of Jim Tooley, who could neither read nor write, but yet had uncanny perceptions in tracking through the bush during the Mau Mau emergency. A running commentary on tiny evidence, inferring what the quarry would do next and proving the hypothesis a few steps further on. Then the ambush, remote in the Kenyan mountains; in the cross-fire a Mau Mau load carrier was hit, and crawled off into the thickets. Tooley followed, and insisted that four fellow soldiers in the Kenya Regiment carry the injured woman over many thousand feet of mountainous scrub to hospital. Was it that sympathy that made his tracking so perceptive? Certainly Anderson, his company commander, thought so.

So our survivors now need rather more than the ability to do one or two special things extremely well. Working in smaller teams is certainly helped by understanding what colleagues know and can contribute. Reacting creatively to changing circumstances requires a well-stocked mind – as Poincaré asserted. Judging what constitutes value in the eyes of a customer is certainly easier if one can identify with his situation, in its economic and personal characteristics. Above all, when so much is changing, personal relationships become crucial.

In 1752, Lord Chesterfield introduced a letter to his son[13] with some advice:

My dear Friend,

I mentioned to you, some time ago, a sentence; which I would most earnestly wish you always to retain in your thoughts, and observe in your conduct. It is *suaviter in modo, fortiter in re*. I do not know any rule so unexceptionably useful and necessary in every part of life.

In other words, a courteous sympathy must go with sound judgement, and determined action. He went on to say,

For my own part, if I bid my footman bring me a glass of wine, in a rough, insulting manner, I should expect, that in obeying me, he would contrive to spill some of it upon me; and I am sure I should deserve it.

Not quite what we would expect of an English magnifico some twenty-five years before the Declaration of Independence, but then Chesterfield was a rather successful statesman. But softness unsupported is not satisfactory either: "A yielding, timid meekness is always abused and insulted by the unjust and the unfeeling; but when sustained by the '*fortiter in re*', is always respected, commonly successful."

When even the largest organisations maintain their strength by favour of their customers, Chesterfield's prescription of gentle manners combined with firmness of mind – a behaviour civil, easy, and frank – must be rather desirable in every individual. Certainly, the abrupt condescension of the bureaucrat, conscious of the unchallengeable power of his organisation, is not sustainable for a moment after his victim realises that a choice exists! Great men can capture the hearts of friends and enemies alike through simple courtesy. Robert E. Lee's sympathy for that wounded union soldier after

Gettysburg must have softened the victor's harshness. Giving the confederate Private Good dinner in his own tent a few weeks later, after an unjust accusation, reinforced the love of his own people.

HAVE FUN!

When the collegiate style, the close co-operation of comrades, is so necessary for success, such a combination of good manners and firm resolve founded on good judgement seems a sound prescription for personal prosperity. Indeed, I have always been struck by the playfulness found in the bright young teams in high technology, whether they are near Cambridge, England, or on the banks of the Charles river. Dave Norton may have trodden "inadvertently" on a colleague's golf ball at a Vermont principals' conference, but his firm leads in the management of information technology for strategic advance. Bostonian Don Laurie's spread-sheets have it there right in the middle: "Have Fun!"; his consultancy has been notably successful in changing attitudes in large corporations, the Scandinavian Airlines System, for example. Even in austere Rome, the most effective headquarters of the ancient world, Horace observed "dulce est desipere in loco" ("it is agreeable to play the fool at the right time")! The favourite toast of the legendary Admiral Halsey is reported by Professor Potter:[14]

> I've drunk your health in company;
> I've drunk your health alone;
> I've drunk your health so many times
> I've damned near ruined my own.

He must have been delighted when a British fleet was assigned to him in the last phase of the war, after the teetotal wardrooms of the US Navy! Potter quotes Admiral Carney on a remarkable collegiate atmosphere:

Halsey ... liked having his staff around him, talking and arguing. He encouraged them to express themselves, regardless of rank. Junior officers never hesitated to disagree sharply with him, his deputy or his chief of staff... Arguments came to an end when Halsey made up his mind."Okay, lads", he would say, "that's it. That's what we'll do."

What a leader! Some great naval figures came from that stable, Admiral Spruance of Battle of Midway fame, for example.

Think how unsuccessful all those grim diligent people were at Woolworths, twelve hours a day, forcing themselves to do yet more – but all fruitless, while their aspect was inward, and their tasks mere procedures. How much better the full-blooded enjoyment so evident in the best led and most successful enterprises in the new fields, never stained by the grim attitudes of bureaucracy: Gordon Edge, of PA Technology, with his private opera; Celltech leading in bio-engineering, with its conversation mall for researchers; and the Boston Ballet's board of enthusiastic entrepreneurs. Sometimes Organisation Man saw something superficially similar, but then more usually a conscious performance of civic responsibility or a manifestation of corporate pomp, rather than the pleasures of companionship that is found in the best teams.

GROW THEM ROUND!

How are these survivors to be formed, so that prospering in a turbulent world is the general experience, rather than one reserved for the exceptionally agile and creative? Not, I think, by narrow education with limited aspirations! "I am the Chairman of the Governors", said the strong voice beside me on the Speech Day platform. "C–O–G; I am a cog, we are all cogs." Quite a shock, with only a minute to go before launching into my speech, with its happy scorn to pour on "cogs turning on their spindles, oblivious of the world beyond their sprockets", and so on. How extraordinary to send young people out into the world of 1988 with that parting message from their schooldays! Surely the survivors need something more to encourage self-development? Can young people safely start their careers expecting their slots and relationships to be as defined as they were thirty years ago? Our first priority must surely be to develop lively citizens, responsible for their own calibre and careers, looking outwards, reacting spontaneously to the new conditions that will surely come their way, as technologies develop, and competitors change.

The old comfortable specialisms, rooted in our schooldays, are just not enough. Certainly in the West, the economic fruits of inventiveness are so often lost, because of those unbridged gaps between individuals formed in specialist moulds. The scientist brought up ignorant of the ways of the commercial world, and the businessmen innocent of the most basic concepts in technology, engineering, and natural science. Computer specialists, polished to be brilliant within their comforting logic, serving their systems like acolytes in a pagan mystery, but unable to conceive the strategic uses for their art, from which the full wealth so often flows. Not so in Japan.

It is the art of integration that survivors need; able to see issues in the round, and draw together several, special strengths in delivering value. Right through a career, managing across the functions is the new necessary skill; wise individuals will seek it out.

WE USED TO

Can we afford to have businesses that are reliant on advanced technology, led by chief executives like that one who lightly remarked that he only once attended a science lesson, and that by accident for ten minutes, until he plucked up courage to withdraw.

When science first developed its commercial significance, our ancestors did not separate its themes from society at large. Recognising, no doubt, that universal geniuses like Leonardo Da Vinci were rare phenomena, yet the Royal Society in its early years brought together scientists and thoughtful laymen, to mutual benefit. Samuel Pepys was an early President, with a voracious interest in navigational science as Secretary to the Navy, but also in a wide range of the liberal arts, as his library in Magdalene College, Cambridge testifies.

With the nineteenth century, came a tremendous movement to channel those powerful new ideas flowing from the scientists into the mainstream of society. In London, that extraordinary man, Count Rumford, founded the Royal Institution with Sir Joseph

Banks, and in 1800 selected Sir Humphrey Davey as its first scientific lecturer. Born Benjamin Thompson in Woburn, Massachusetts, Rumford showed in his career some of the diversity of interest that his Royal Institution still shows today. Scientist, soldier, gardener, and expert on smoking chimneys, Rumford was created a Count of the Holy Roman Empire by a grateful King of Bavaria, and knighted by George III. In those early years, the Royal Institution packed its beautiful lecture theatre with society people, to hear Davey, inventor of the miner's lamp, Faraday – and Samuel Taylor Coleridge. Throughout the country, over the next forty years, several hundred institutions were set up by local citizens with the same objectives – to bring science and society closer together, and to help individuals from all walks of life feel friendly with that powerful new phenomenon, scientific knowledge. Athenaeums, Philosophical Societies, Literary and Scientific Institutions, Mechanics Institutes, some 600 in all, open to everyone. Now less than a dozen remain, and the Royal Institution, still with its Friday evening discourses for a black tie and long dress audience. Is the need less, or have the two cultures become dangerously separated? In Britain the answer must be yes to the second.

SOME DO STILL

In the United States the condition seems more hopeful. Benjamin Franklin's kite and Paul Revere's magnificent silver presentation pitcher from the Boston Mechanic Association are images to remind us how the young Republic took science into society at large, and not just for the philosophers. New York University was founded after a Convention of Literary and Scientific Gentlemen, meeting together in the Common Council Chamber of the City of New York, as the proceedings, published in 1831, inform us.[15] The letter of invitation, 25 September 1830, included:

In contemplating the various plans, by which the University, as well as other seminaries of learning in our country, might best promote their common cause, it has been thought, that a meeting of literary and scientific gentlemen, to confer on the general interests of letters and liberal education, would be attended with happy results.

Impressed with the belief that our literary men, and literary institutions, have been too much insulated, it is urged that more frequent intercourse and comparison of views, would be a source of high gratification to all, and a benefit to those interested in the welfare of science and literature.

Among those who gave papers was Lt. Mahan, aged twenty-eight, Professor of Engineering at West Point, father to the great naval historian.

That tradition prospers still, and though for a time leading institutions like Harvard and Stanford fell for the prevailing fallacy of vocational specialisation, they are back now with their traditional concern to educate balanced minds. Princeton never strayed; perhaps absorbing the dire message of *Organisation Man* better than most, since that book was written by an alumnus. In the 1970s, when specialisation was all the rage elsewhere, no Princeton man could gain his bachelor's degree without at least two semesters in each of the four main streams; science, arts and letters, history and politics, social science and economics. Then the selected major subject for the last two years. Intriguingly, while proficiency in at least one language was required too, Latin or Aramaic were quite acceptable. The physics for poets courses, now sadly less colourfully named contemporary physics, were noted for the eminence of the lecturers; Nobel prizewinners seemed to enjoy the freshness of treatment needed to capture the liberal mind.

For such a broad education to be possible at university, American children need protection from early specialisation, and in the best schools they get it. Whatever their academic characteristics, every one of the 900 or so young people graduating in 1974 from the New Trier Township High School north of Chicago, had studied mathematics, science, English, history, and a language right to the end of their schooling at eighteen. More than 90 per cent of those young people moved on to further education. That was not a selected elite; every child living in the communities of Wilmette, Winnetka, Kenilworth, Glencoe went to the New Trier schools, which were run by a locally elected and financed school board.

William Whyte's warning of 1957 is working, then, in the United

States education system; those that strayed are returning to the path, and we can observe a society in which the barriers to mutual understanding among the young are fruitfully low. Not low enough in later life, though, as indignant technologists protest at the scientific illiteracy of a Secretary of Defense, for example. But scientists too have a responsibility to be understood! The separation of attitudes caused by the specialisms of the feudal corporation undo much of the mutual understanding of the new graduate. There are cohesive forces; the classless American accent, the emphasis on nation building that draws new immigrants into the fold, and the spirit of the Constitution all seem to promote an easy interchange of ideas – at least to a British observer, aware of the barriers that rampant specialisation, combined with a coterie culture, can buttress.

That the United States has an education problem is evident, but surely it lies primarily in the inner cities, and the peculiarly American freedom for the inadequate to decline further in the midst of affluence. Twenty miles south of the New Trier School Board's admirable service, south Chicago's problems seem insuperable. The American system reinforces success in education, and redoubles the problems of the failing. Wealthier families move out to districts that offer good schools, and bring their taxes and support to help those schools get better still. Meanwhile, poor schooling in the inner city makes family housing less attractive to the affluent, depressing prices. The housing then attracts the less well off and the new immigrants; southwest Chicago has seen a tremendous influx of hispanic speakers in the past twenty years, bringing awesome new education tasks, and less local taxable income to meet them. Fortunately President Bush has declared that his will be an Education Presidency!

In continental Europe some of the healthy philosophy seen in the United States has deep roots. The baccalaureate, feared by every generation of French young as they approach eighteen, does insist that each one of them demonstrates knowledge on a broad front at the point that they leave school. But then a strange system allows unlimited enrolment for courses in further education, leaving the first-year examinations to wreak frightful havoc among young people who have chosen too ambitiously for their capabilities. Nevertheless, French men and women are educated to the end of their schooldays on a broad plan, and that seems to promote a fruitful flow of ideas to and fro. In the higher echelons, the broad education of the elite in the *Grandes Écoles* makes for a mutual understanding among policy makers that should be envied everywhere outside Japan, where Tokyo University seems to produce a similar effect.

OTHERS TRY!

In Britain, there are some grounds for hope; adoption of the national curriculum is certainly encouraging. If every child really gets 15 per cent or so of schooling in science and technology from the age of five to sixteen, we can perhaps expect to see science back in the body of social experience – ending that separation of the cultures that has so damaged Britain's ability to harvest economic fruit from the astounding creativity of its scientists.

Encouragingly, too, the science curriculum calls for heavy emphasis on scientific method and philosophies, as well as the facts themselves – which can look dated so soon. If honest observation, inference and hypothesis become commonplace in the new generation, we should certainly see a nation of survivors in a turbulent world. Perhaps that cardinal virtue among scientists – rejecting favourite but untenable hypotheses – will become pervasive too; Thomas Huxley's "great tragedy of Science – the slaying of a beautiful hypothesis by an ugly fact".[16] The disposition that seeks to test comfortable and loved attitudes, and rejects them when proved false, will surely help survival, provided that the creative urge to form new and more resilient hypotheses is there as well.

LIBERAL EDUCATION: LUXURY OR NECESSITY?

If schools have fostered the desire to specialise, allowing young people to drop the uncomfortable subject, preparation for work has accentuated the separations. Driven by the Victorian concept of the professional man, honed further by Organisation Man's urge to narrow skill, most processes for forming young people have cut them off from the broader concepts that are so important when working in small teams, and in rapidly changing circumstances. People who started careers a few years ago, confident that their first employer would carry them through to retirement, now know that is unlikely. Their first faith, that the employer would see that they would learn what they needed to know, was based on a fallacy; their longer-term interests may not be coincident. Most people will change employment at least once in a career, and those that stay will find the work they will do quite different from the work they were trained to do. The wide support among individuals for the new British system of management education suggests that a crucial lesson has gone home; calibre and competence are primarily of personal concern. Of course, wise employers know that competent managers create more wealth, but as loyalties become more temporary, the wise individual will plan his own development.

Forming individuals with the broader insights and sure touch needed in changing circumstances, calls for more than continuing formal education; those skills are learnt from experience too. The British Army develops its young officers through the jobs they are given, with education added from time to time. Specialist, staff, and line commands all play their part in developing the well-formed individual – the "ad unguem factus homo", as Horace described Maecenas. I advise my own children to seek career steps that open options, not close them. So comfortable for an employer to let a skilled person rest in a post calling for special skills. So comfortable, but so damaging to the future prospects of that individual. I recall one able executive in BT, capable of high command, but for years backwatered as a satellite specialist. Left in that field, he could never have explored the full potential of his personality; reluctant to move, pleased now perhaps, as his career develops.

HELP THEM BOUNCE

Surely, some might say, the survivors in these new battlefields will be as scarce and shell-shocked as the remnants of a Vietnam firefight. What about the stress? All very well for the few gallant and resilient souls who smile through anything, but what about the great majority – those who can survive as cogs, but feel lost as free agents in a jungle war. Perhaps that is the point; ordinary people, a cross-section of society, can not only survive, but triumph victoriously over danger and turmoil – provided they are well trained, and well led. And within that art of leadership lies the talent to judge what responsibilities an individual can rise to, and the generosity to give the clear authority needed to complete the task. Remember Admiral Mahan's observations on Nelson's leadership style (p. 118)? How different when responsibility is forced down, without the power to decide; surely that is the nutcracker that breaks the spirit? All very well if you have procedures to fall back on, because then at least you have the bureaucrat's defence!

Pressure to achieve results no doubt works very well when the criteria for action can be clearly defined in advance – sending a battalion over the top in the battle of the Somme, for example. But how well does such pressure work when success calls for sympathy, creativity, and co-operation – as well as the bulldog qualities of tenacity and diligence? Then inspiration rather than coercion is surely the key; competence and responsibility the watchwords.

Notes

1 Tacitus, *Annalium: Liber VI*, ed. Ryckius (Hackius, Leiden, 1687), p. 160.
2 W. H. Whyte, *The Organisation Man* (Cape, London, 1957).
3 Leo Tolstoy, *War and Peace*, tr. Constance Garnett (Heinemann, London, 1971), p. 849.
4 David Chandler, *The Campaigns of Napoleon* (Weidenfeld & Nicolson, London, 1978), p. 805.
5 A. T. Mahan, *The Influence of Sea Power upon the French Revolution and Empire* (Little, Brown; Boston, 1894), p. 274.
6 Julius Caesar, *De Bello Gallico: Commentarius II*, ed. T. Rice Holmes (Medici, London, 1913), p. 48.
7 Henri Poincaré, *Science et Méthode* (Flammarion, Paris, 1908), p. 60.
8 Dugald Stewart, *Elements of the Philosophy of the Human Mind* (Cadell, Davies, Creech; London and Edinburgh, 1802), p. 320.
9 Joshua Reynolds, *Discourses* (Cadell, London, 1778), p. 211.
10 J. L. Lowes, *The Road to Xanadu* (Constable, London, 1930).
11 Reynolds, *Discourses*, p. 207.

12 Alan Ritter, *Anarchism* (Cambridge University Press, Cambridge, 1980), p. 56.
13 Earl of Chesterfield, *Letters to his Son*, vol. III (Dodsley, London, 1774), p. 133.
14 E. B. Potter, *Bull Halsey* (Naval Institute Press, Annapolis, 1988), p. 245.
15 *Journal of the Proceedings of a Convention of Literary and Scientific Gentlemen*, (Leavitt, Carvill, New York, 1831).
16 T. H. Huxley, *Collected Essays*, vol. VIII (Macmillan, London, 1908), p. 244.

9

THE NEW LEADERSHIP

THE PASSING OF AUTOCRACY

THE feudal world, with its strong sense of structure and reverence for the authority of its leaders, certainly did not encourage debate on their dicta. Just as Marcus Terentius sardonically remarked to the Emperor Tiberius, the glory of obedience characterised that social form. In 1655, Louis XIV could say "L'état c'est moi"; but while the divine right of kings held sway, it was for most fear that forced that conformity, as Vaclav Havel helps us to appreciate, in his wry satires on the communist social cage.

But it was not like that in the heroic age: Agamemnon, about to lift the siege of Troy, faced this onslaught from young Diomedes, in Homer's words, translated by Alexander Pope.[1]

> If I oppose thee, Prince! thy Wrath with-hold,
> The Laws of Council bid my Tongue be bold ...
> The Gods have made thee but by halves a King;
> They gave thee Sceptres, and a wide Command,
> They gave Dominion o'er the Seas and Land,
> The noblest Pow'r that might the World controul
> They gave thee not – a brave and virtuous Soul.

A rather tolerant chief executive to bear with that outburst; perhaps his pleasure in finding a fighting spirit in his army compensated for the offence to his *amour propre*.

In that age of the individual, even Olympus saw questioning of the supreme authority, reflecting the values of men. Jove had his problems. In a full board meeting of the gods he laid down corporate policy: no interference with either side in the battle for Troy, under penalty of being fixed with burning chains to brazen floors in hell. To no effect. His own wife, Juno, "headstrong and imperious still, she claims some title to transgress his will," wheedles the head of a major subsidiary – Neptune – to join the war on the side of her favourite Greeks; she borrows Venus' marvellous girdle to infatuate her husband. The old chairman, moved by the unaccustomed caress nods off, waking in fury to find that some of his directors have launched an enterprise while he dozed. Neptune leading the Greeks in battle, and the Trojans in full retreat. A corporate aide is sent hot foot to insist on instant compliance with board policy, to be met with:[2]

> What means the haughty Sov'reign of the Skies,
> (The King of Ocean thus, incens'd, replies)
> Rule as he will his portion'd Realms on high;
> No Vassal God, nor of his Train am I.

How reminiscent of a modern boardroom! Does not Neptune's reply have its echo in the Crocker president's reaction to control from the Midland Bank in London, or Sohio's chairman and BP?

That breezy contest for power survived only in pockets when feudal structures dominated a society that was terrified by incessant marauding after the collapse of the Roman Empire; then, when people hungered after order, the sacred authority of the appointed ruler was held to justify passive obedience in some very disagreeable regimes. Even the great William the Silent, founder of Holland out of the empire of Philip II, was deeply concerned at the illegitimacy of his new state. It took three revolutions to bury that concept in the West: 1688, 1776, and 1789. A regrowth of absolutism after the defeat of Napoleon was finally routed in 1848, when all Europe rose against the remaining feudalists, with remarkably coincident uprisings in Paris, Rome, Vienna, Cracow, Naples, and Turkey. The United States gained Texas, California, and much else from a Mexico troubled by the instability of the old world.

SET THEM FREE!

The rigidity of the feudal world started to crack much earlier where individual freedom was well rooted. First in Italy, then in the Low Countries and in Britain, the Renaissance saw new styles of leadership emerge, after the long centuries of autocratic and unquestioned authority. In the turbulent sixteenth century, Queen Elizabeth sent men and ships out with only the most general objectives – relying on initiative and a healthy instinct for self-enrichment. Britain's huge empire made its most dramatic advances under the inspiration of the elder Pitt. In that *annus mirabilis* 1759, fleets and armies thousands of miles apart scored victory after victory, within the strategy of a supreme command, but through the creative aggression of individual leaders close to the opportunity, with the power to act on their own judgement. James Wolfe at Quebec, Boscawen at Quiberon Bay, the battles of Minden and Madras, saw victories inconceivable if planned in detail from above or directed from the centre. Forty years later, Nelson's "perfect and generous confidence" in his captains made his victories possible too.

Of course those changes, in the balance of individual freedom and in the structure of society, took decades to evolve. In our corporate world, the swift onset of turbulence has caught some leaders on the hop; they have found the pace too fast. When giants like ITT and GEC have won stock market praise for twenty years through tight control of costs and contracts, it cannot be easy to find new ways of leading.

THE NEW AGENDA

New conditions demand a fresh approach. As the monoliths and structured hierarchies prove arthritic in the fast new game, empowering the individual is the new requirement, to act with personal initiative, close to the opportunity. No longer is it sound for the leader to insist that all is done his way; delegation means that others will find ways of doing things that may seem odd to the rule-maker, but, if relevant, prompt and energetic, more likely to win. Perhaps de Tocqueville's observation will console, "La liberté démocratique ... fait moins bien chaque chose, mais elle fait plus de choses."[3]

No longer can the general hope to see every detail of the battle from his command post; it just is not feasible for even the most active leader of a complex business to have a hand on every lever. Not possible to do so and yet vitalise the team; not practical to juggle with a fast-moving present and judge calmly the imponderable forces affecting the future. When direct action by the leader himself is more rarely appropriate, the new man must achieve through the will of others. Success will go now to the *impresario*, skilled in generating the enthusiasm and focusing the aspirations of many individuals with distinct talents. He listens, sensitive to the breath of new influence; he shapes, aware that people need a vision and a structure; he inspires in each an urge to excel, when the criteria of that excellence are relative to external standards, specific in each case. Leadership in turbulence is an affair of the whole human being, with the statistics and the specialists on tap but not on top, as the saying goes.

When the leader has devolved the authority to decide, and can no longer see all the action; when the proven rulebook may be obsolete before it is printed; he must find new ways to achieve his goals. The direct order is replaced by a framework – a set of values to guide the independent actions of many individuals. Devising that framework needs sympathetic thought, specific to the objective, because the crucial concern is what people will do under the influence of those formulae. Principles that look sound from the boardroom, or have been proved valid in different circumstances, may cause strange effects in other conditions, or when other personal criteria operate. Frameworks formed for a predictable world can hold fallacies in turbulence.

SOME FALLACIES

Short-term financial controls, so loved by the institutional investor and those who only feel safe in the firm shuffle forward, can surely damage basic strengths in any business, if not countervailed by longer-term strategic thrusts. There are so many ways that the ambitious executive can sacrifice future opportunities, so as to score well in the next quarterly review. In banking, making risky loans at high rates will show excellent immediate results, until those borrowers fail, first to pay the interest charges, and then to refund the capital. In manufacturing, the temptation to shave the budget for research and development can be hard to resist if the inquisition at corporate HQ is concerned only with measurable returns, now. In some businesses – aerospace and electronics, for example – 6 or 7 per cent of sales may need to be invested in new information systems and automation, to match a competitor's speed of development, or to steal a march in factory flexibility. How easy to spend a little longer commissioning reports and evaluating the alternatives – if today's profits still look good to the accountants at head office. After all, there is always the chance of promotion, leaving a successor to justify the new expenditures when they are inescapable, and to explain falling market share and narrow profit margins. No, leadership through short-term financial controls alone is far too dangerous for any organisation in turbulence, where neglect of the sinews for future battles can lead to extinction.

It used to happen in Japan; Tohatsu in the early 1950s had 22 per cent of the motorcycle market, earned 8 per cent after tax on sales, with moderate debt. Theirs was a disciplined conservative leadership, concentrating on short-term results. In five years Honda smashed them into bankruptcy, through aggressive product development. After sacrificing their own short term to build competitive force, Honda seized a rich harvest: their net profit rose from 3.4 per cent to 10.3 per cent, and market share from 20 per cent to 44 per cent. When Yamaha tried the reverse trick in 1982, Honda responded ferociously: executives were not held to their quarterly ratios, but inspired to drive through 113 product changes in eighteen months – transforming their entire product range twice. Yamaha were forced down from 37 per cent to 23 per cent of the market, selling motor bikes below cost in desperation. David Montgomery sets out the tale in his Stanford research paper.[4] When times are turbulent, the more powerfully pressures are applied to individuals in the grip of short-term controls, the sooner catastrophe will occur, and the more complete the destruction that follows. Strategic victory requires strategic vision and strategic investment.

Organisations in which power is devolved are peculiarly prone to fallacies, if no one takes the trouble to conceive what general implications may flow from apparently innocent causes – the resident pathogens, as Professor Reason calls them;[5] characteristics of behaviour that are induced unexpectedly by value systems and procedures, sometimes with catastrophic results. Where many individuals act on their own initiative, the decision rules they follow are obviously crucial. The successful new leader's first priority must be to hunt out those fallacies and correct them.

Perhaps the most pervasive cause of strategic error over the past thirty years has been that most cherished of all financial tools – the calculation of Discounted Cash Flow (DCF), or Net Present Value as the modern financial fashion would have it. Adopted by the British government's Treasury in the 1960s, that framework for decisions has influenced all aspects of government and commercial activity. The very power and efficiency of a finance function makes the effects of an inherent fallacy there both pervasive and irresistible. The introduction of DCF, first made fashionable in George Brown's national plan of 1964, enshrined in mathematical form the focus on short-term financial performance, so strong a feature of decision making today. Discounting by 8 or 10 per cent each year the future value of an asset, DCF has proved to be a formula for pillaging posterity; the rights of our successors may be diminished to extinction. When 3 to 4 per cent real return on an investment has been the norm over long periods of history, the eager demand for much higher returns in pursuit of the superlative investment merely devalues those assets that bring benefits to our successors. According to the formula, an asset that would be worth £1 million today, may rate less than a tenth of that value if the harvest is delayed for a generation. No wonder forests have been laid low around the world, replanted – if replanted they are – by quick-growing softwoods, with the earliest possible harvest time. How different the wealth in beauty and infrastructure that we have inherited from ancestors less greedy than ourselves.

Discounted Cash Flow as generally applied contains another fallacy too; an unused asset is usually calculated to have the same real value at a future date, before the discount is applied – or even diminished, for the sake of prudence. That assumption is clearly fallacious for a limited resource. I am pleased to recall that when, in 1968, McKinsey were considering the preferred extraction rate for gas from the North Sea, we did recognise that 2.4 old pence per therm might look a little cheap in twenty-five years' time, even after general inflation! So at least in that major industry, common sense was allowed to prevail over economic fashion.

In my next major industry, the formula for assessing major investment options contained a further fallacy, just as damaging. Telecommunications in the 1970s, just delivered from the main body of the Civil Service, gave Treasury rules an unfortunate twist. In refusing to give credit for customer benefits enjoyed but not paid for, a generation of network equipment offered less to the customer in improved service than the technology was capable of providing. After all, if an improvement in quality or reliability cost money, but only saved maintenance costs for the monopoly, most such improvements would be eliminated under the sharp pencil of the evaluating team.

Almost universal in organisations of the predictable world, is the fallacy of introversion. Budgets for specialists and the incentive bonus combine to drive already inward looking people to optimise on their own narrow criteria, whatever the effect on the rest of the process. British Telecom used to divide the purchasing organisation from supply; no wonder we had splendid contracts, and ran out of essential spares. New orders for telephone sets were generated automatically from the figures for issues from stores, rather than orders from customers; no wonder we finished up with ever larger stocks of the colours no one wanted – as temporary loans, until the right ones arrived, triggered yet further purchases of unwanted equipment. Those facility managers in Woolworths may have saved money on lighting their stores, but scarcely helped sales, if customers could not see the merchandise. The boundary between two proud baronies in the old corporate hierarchies, has always proved a happy hunting ground for the fallacy sleuth!

ARCHITECTURE FOR HARMONY

If the first task is to hunt existing fallacies and correct them, leaders
of disaggregated organisations certainly need structure – frameworks
within which the multitude of individual decisions can yet be compatible, where that is important. In a very large technical project
like the development of System X, with 2,500 engineers working
on fourteen major sub-systems, it was obviously crucial to define
precisely the interfaces between separate system elements, so that
when they came together they worked. Now, with information
crucial to everyone, it is not just high technology companies that
need technology architectures. If information systems are developed
by devolved business units – as they should be – they will combine
for the corporate benefit only if they are designed within an architecture that specifies the hardware, the communication interfaces,
the software languages, and the form in which data are collected
and stored. Defining those aspects of the system scarcely limit the
inventive freedom of the individual, but they are certainly needed
if that freedom is not to result in a cacophonous babble. In IBM,
only 2 per cent of information system specialists work for the
central function; the rest apply themselves to the priorities of trading
divisions.

One key task of those people at the centre is to create an architecture that not only keeps harmony among the various baronial
systems throughout the empire, but is also capable of building
commercial strength outside the business. IBM did that rather well,
with their proprietary System Network Architecture, until their
competitors joined in establishing the new public protocol known
as Open Systems Interconnect, now well on its way to being the
recognised standard in Europe and America. General Motors' introduction of a proprietary standard reflected a desire too to see that
the outside world adopted systems compatible with their own.
Where suppliers, designers, and distributors each conform to the
requirements of a technology architecture, an immense, ramified
network can be created through initiatives of independent parties,
and yet be harmonious and internally compatible.

To be effective, architectures need the commitment of firm leadership. Where that is absent, definitions can be loose and harmony

lost. In telecommunications, for example, the present international standard allows for two incompatible digital systems. The fifty-six kilobit frame in North America, and the sixty-four kilobit system in Britain and most of the world. That permissive definition can scarcely be called a standard! Fortunately, a Europe that has shown the desire to work as a team is causing its own standard to prevail, with all the benefits that can bring in advanced services and markets for terminal equipment. The imprecision of standards regulating military material in NATO is more serious still. With operational needs overridden by national political considerations, NATO armed forces are equipped with munitions that fit their own equipment – but not their neighbours'; the smooth bore German tank gun, for example, cannot fire the shells needed by the rifled British version. The need for each national contingent to retire or advance along its own lines of communication could prove embarrassing in a fluid war.

BREATHING LIFE

With fallacies removed, minds turned outwards, and architecture to condition relationships between self-sparking individuals, the new leader has called a halt to self-destruction, and to the advance of anarchy. Next must come the vitality and convergence of effort that only an inspiring strategy can produce. Just like Pitt in the eighteenth century and Templer in Malaya, the leader's strong vision is needed to turn the disaggregated organisation from an investment trust into a victorious enterprise. We have some notable examples to observe.

Walter Wriston, for twelve years at the head of Citicorp, relentlessly pursued his vision of the modern financial empire, on which the sun never sets; a business in which fees earned from services would exceed the traditional interest on funds lent out – added value without the risk of bad debt. Recognising the importance of seconds in information about money, he caused his people to create systems linking his decision makers around the world, passing from London to New York and on again to Tokyo the task of adjusting the group's financial exposure round the clock, responding globally to market reactions wherever they occur. With customer databases related, financial exposure to groups of customers can be tracked, and marketing leads identified. Services to customers could draw on every scrap of information held in the bank. Wriston's vision was not received wisdom when he formed it, and was still being criticised by competitors just as the commercial strength was about to be demonstrated. Citicorp today is the result of that vision; still no doubt capable of error, but less liable to ignorance than most.

Digital Corporation had a visionary leader too in Olsen. He saw that his business was creating through its processor technology a chain of added value, but was leaving others to harvest the richest fruit. Again, over a decade his vision drove Digital to pursue that added value around the world. First the computer systems built round those processors, then the application software and the enjoyable margins and predictable earnings of the fixed-term maintenance contract. Now, more than half Digital's growth in profits comes from service businesses that only a few years ago were beyond the corporate fence. That transformation too came from a clear vision, relentlessly applied over years.

In Japan, a phalanx of powerful competitors leaped still further forward through dedication to dazzling product innovation and fast reaction to market tremors: Sony, Matsushita, Sharp, Toyota, Hitachi, NEC, Toshiba, Honda, and Hino are all included in George Stalk's list of time-conscious companies, using advanced information technology to slash development times, make factories flexible at short notice, and allow each customer's order to be handled in days rather than weeks. Strategies that harness every aspect of a business's relationships inside and out, to deliver dramatic competitive power, sacrificing short-term results if need be, as Honda showed in its merciless fight with Yamaha.

Indeed, consistency of vision seems crucial in a large corporation, and desirable everywhere. The absurdity of fine tuning the course in a devolved organisation, or worst still in a traditional structure, is most obvious to those who receive the signals: order, counter-order, disorder. The leader must surely adapt the length of his stride to the complexity of his organisation. Just as a cathedral can turn speech at ordinary pace into gibberish whatever the amplification, as speech paths cross and reverberate, so a large organisation contains within it the themes of a decade – with old phrases gradually diminishing in significance as new ones gain force, if repeated frequently and consistently.

THE WELL TEMPERED LEADER

Above all, in a turbulent age the new leader needs judgement. When the past is only an uncertain guide to the future, he needs the intellect to conceive what forces bear upon his future, and the personality to judge soberly the capability for action. Those must be crucial characteristics in a leader who can take his enterprise consistently to victory. Joseph Addison gives us the sublime picture of the Duke of Marlborough at Blenheim, "he ... rides in the whirlwind, and directs the storm".[6] That image of the sure-footed leader, vital yet serene amidst turbulence, all-seeing and calm in judgement, certainly won the loyalty of those mixed battalions of Dutch, German, and British soldiers who stemmed the power of the Sun King. "Marlborough never lost a battle, because he never fought a battle he could not win." That was the phrase I used to modify the eagerness of some rash telecom managers in challenging the piecemeal aggression of our trade unions in the 1979 "winter of discontent".

The Roman Empire found itself embroiled in serious wars through local folly – the arrogance of young Appius Claudius in Armenia, for example, or Crassus' avarice for Parthian gold.[7] Controlling the hotheads is more crucial in some instances than in others – certainly no wise leader is happy to find energies locked in needless battles, which may be lost. How to prevent such follies has vexed empires, and should concern also the wise leader of a disaggregated organisation, though Wu Ch'i perhaps went too far, in ordering the execution of the warrior who dashed forward from the line of battle and slew the enemy's champion in single combat.[8]

More admirable is that combination of tactical skill, judgement, and the ability to coalesce the intentions of individuals that Marlborough demonstrated on the battlefields of Europe in the first decade of the eighteenth century. Time and again he manœuvred to present the allies with an opportunity for victory, only to find that one element or another of his force held back: the Dutch field deputies, the Margrave of Baden, or perhaps one of his own units arrived too late. Without complaint, where he judged the force available was not sufficient to achieve his objective, he withdrew, regrouped, and manœuvred for another opportunity. When the tactical position was sound, and he judged that his forces were coherent and sufficient for victory, he struck hard. I found those precepts helpful in the less glorious task of wresting the control of Britain's international telephone service from union activists. A careful campaign of meas-ures, developed over eighteen months and more, agreed with James Hodgson, head of the international executive, and his colleagues, seized the initiative and kept it. When the time was right, the frontline management acted firmly to put the new procedures in place, secure in the knowledge that my signature had authorised their stand, and that this time, they would not be abandoned under pressure. The union called a stoppage: they walked as far as the door, and turned back. The confidence of victory in firstline management settled the issue. A confidence that was not derived from the reckless "do your worst" defiance; a confidence that was built on the sure knowledge of necessary actions soundly conceived and solidly backed.

THE FIRST VICTORY IS SWEETEST

Every leader of free men and women needs to establish that he brings victory with him. Field Marshal Bramall, one of Britain's most thoughtful soldiers, urges a general in a new command to organise victory as the first priority. Even setting a brigade against a company position may be justified, if it brings that first sense that the new leader is a winner. Certainly Montgomery, criticised by some for excessive caution, knew that the mystique of Field Marshal Rommel could only be cleared from the minds of the Eighth Army if his own initial actions resulted in solid victories. At Alam Halfa, and then Alamein, he certainly produced those. In 1979, Sainsbury's Depot Replenishment program set their corporate computer system on the path to success.

Marlborough had shown his generation of leaders that it was not cowardly to refuse battle in which defeat was probable; providing that the will to re-engage was there. Sir Richard Grenville's suicidal attack in the *Revenge* on the mass Spanish fleet in Queen Elizabeth's time, may have made for stirring ballads, but would have destroyed his country, had he a fleet to commit, rather than a single small ship. One of the great heroes in Rome's wars with Hannibal, Fabius Maximus Cunctator, was given his cognomen – The Delayer – in admiration for the series of indecisive actions in which he weakened the power of his adversary while never exposing his own forces to destruction. Marshal Kutuzoff's controlled retreat before Napoleon led to the destruction of that disturber of mankind.

ANOTHER WAY

A very modern leader who developed his style from left-wing views in youth is Sir Peter Thompson, of the British National Freight Consortium. The extraordinary growth of that rag-bag of nationalised transportation businesses is one of the epics of our time. Bought from the government by its employees in 1980, the next eight years saw share prices increase 100-fold, making truck drivers into millionaires. How was it done? Structure, strategy, and style. With his 30,000 employees grouped into 700 business units, no one feels very far from the customer or from the profit and loss account. With thousands of substantial employee shareholders, poor performers get short shrift. Protestors from a disbanded unit at the Annual General Meeting were disconcerted to find that their protests were not met by brotherly support in the union spirit, but by critical rejection. "You've had your come-uppance", from fellow workers who had observed slack performance and disapproved.

Peter Thompson, though, brought something more; he brought a strategy founded on values perceived by the customer, rather than the traditional introverted concern with internal transport functions. "Sell solutions not features", is said to be the IBM cry. Certainly, selling solutions – the whole task, end to end – has paid off well for National Freight. Nowhere more so than in moving business families around the world, where the transfer of a household, entire and breakage free, looks very much like value; usually each element in the complex process just looks like hassle. In distributing the *Financial Times*, taking responsibility for the whole chain – printer to

newsagent – looks like value too, particularly when the system
seems free of union sanctions.

Recognising that employing shareholders is fine while stock prices
rise, but disagreeable in retreat, National Freight starts its mission
statement with "we'll seek to become a company for all seasons".
Structure and strategy, but perhaps most important, style. With
main board members each nursing a constituency of employee
shareholders, with good performance seen as a social duty, National
Freight's remarkable financial achievement can only have come
from superb development of individual capabilities. A humane style
with practical economic benefits: why, it even pays off in making
acquisitions, when owners accept a lower price from a congenial
suitor. Quite a formula! Generous bonuses each year, related to
achievement against budget, are a feature of the style too; focusing
attention on the business unit rather than the remote corporation.
Twelve and a half per cent on basic pay for achieving quality, and
30 per cent more for getting the financials right, gives some balance
between the short term, and building the long-term assets of goodwill and reputation.

Does this all sound a bit like a Yugoslavian co-operative? Is it a
formula that only works on the way up, a frustrating encumbrance
when Icarus heads for the water? Perhaps, but maybe not. After all,
the power of those worker shareholders lies in the Annual General
Meeting, and in the election of directors. Once named, they can be
backed or sacked. While in the saddle, they are free to act, unlike
those unfortunate leaders in the communist world who have to fight
individual issues through an Athenian democracy. In Athens the
Agora, fraught with every citizen, paralysed the power of Demos-
thenes to resist Philip of Macedon, who could make his own
decisions fast. Democracy has its many forms; some give the inspiration of freedom, while harnessing the individual to the common
good; others debilitate.

THE PERSONAL TOUCH

Developing frameworks and systems to motivate in the devolved
organisation does not reduce the need for that personal inspiration

that has been the hallmark of great leaders through history. Certainly, when radical change is in the air, the conviction that the new ways have the backing of a real person ambitious for victory, rather than some committee of psychologists or behavioural scientists, can be comforting. Disembodied manipulation is repugnant, in any cause. So, for years in BT, I set aside one day every week to visit the field. To dine with the senior managers, debate with the juniors; climb up a telephone pole, and down a manhole; visit the exchanges and talk to the unions. Those visits surely confirmed that the new values were there to stay; they certainly provided an agreeable break from the stream of unresolved problems that finish inevitably on the top desk. Such a relief to be reminded that good things are being done, as a change from those "disgusted" letters, with copies to Members of Parliament.

BORN OR MADE?

If successful leadership comes in so many forms, how should leaders be developed? And developed they must be, though some romantics may believe leadership falls like divine grace on a blessed few; or, in Montgomery's sardonic phrase, like dew from heaven. First, as he showed, great leaders need to be competent. Great charisma will get men or women to follow you once; but perhaps next time they will remember whether their trust was fruitful, or ended in chaos and tears. Competence brings too that sense of capability and resource that can foster resilience and creativity. Just as Poincaré told us,[9] facts need to be in the subconscious to feed the imagination.

Most successful leaders, in a world that requires so much of them, will be individuals with rather broader capabilities than their predecessors. No longer just committee-men, for as Donald Petersen of Ford Motor Company put it to a Californian audience in 1988, intuition and emotion must count in successful market judgements. For that, formation needs to start early; open to mathematics, science, and technology, but also to the humane studies. That the obviously practical subjects are not enough is a cause that needs more defenders. Corelli Barnett may be winning too great a victory.

Leadership, though, is more than just a matter of the intellect.

While the connection between the playing fields of Eton and mastery of the British Empire may be a little strained, leadership does seem to be a skill that works best when unselfconscious. And if unselfconscious, best surely learnt in early youth. Squash and fencing may stir the competitive instincts, but for leadership the team game is the thing – and the newest team game of all for the young is the business venture. In Britain, 25,000 teenagers join together each year in groups of ten or so to form a business, float the shares, prosper or stagnate, and then back to base, liquidation and final dividends. Young Enterprise is an extraordinary national movement with incalculable benefits for the leadership talents of young people. Football, hockey, and cricket nurture leaders too, and sparkling individualists. But the thousands of young people trying their hand at a commercial enterprise perhaps learn something more: they learn the art of the balanced judgement.

WHOSE RESPONSIBILITY?

For most, the power to lead is one developed over years, inspired by others, reassured by success. Not, I think, an affair exclusively for the training department or the classroom. Leaders develop leaders. In the days of Organisation Man, there was a specialist for everything: even for management development. Paradoxically, in the era of delegation there are some things the prudent chief executive takes to himself; he is not just the conductor of an orchestra, for example, playing off another man's score. Corporate strategy used to be an affair for the specialists; now no prudent leader leaves that task to others. Organisation structure and appointments used to be the preserve of the personnel function; but not, I think, in today's most successful companies. Financial controls were devised by accountants; but look at the appalling consequences of fallacies in misguided zeal. But of all the tasks that truly belong to the new chief executive, the development of leaders can least be left to the *apparatchiks*. Leaders must develop leaders.

NOTES

1 Homer, *The Iliad*, vol. III, tr. Alexander Pope (Lintott, London, 1717), p. 5.
2 Ibid., vol. IV, p. 170.
3 Alexis de Tocqueville, *De la Démocratie en Amérique*, vol. II (Gosselin, Paris, 1835), p. 131.
4 David B. Montgomery, "Understanding the Japanese as customers, competitors, and collaborators", Research Paper, Stanford University (April 1989).
5 James Reason, "The contribution of latent human failures to the breakdown of complex systems", *Philosophic Transactions of the Royal Society* (1990).
6 Joseph Addison, *The Campaign* (1705).
7 A. N. Sherwin-White, *Roman Foreign Policy in the East* (Duckworth, London, 1984), pp. 174 and 279–290.
8 Sun Tzu, *The Art of War*, tr. Samuel B. Griffith (Oxford University Press, Oxford, 1971), p. 107.
9 Henri Poincaré, *Science et Méthode* (Flammarion, Paris, 1908).

10

MANAGING RISK

DELEGATE, DON'T ABDICATE!

IT is a happy paradox that the technology that brought turbulence to the world of work, and the need to devolve decisions to many individuals, also brought the means to do so prudently. In 1970 I saw how one big British bank controlled the activities of its dealers in Eurobonds and other securities. In a large room, a small army of men and women busy on the telephone, recorded their transactions on paper. "How do you know what all those deals add up to?" I asked the director in charge. "Oh that's quite straightforward, back to back," he said. When any one of those dealers found a customer wishing to borrow $1 million for six months, say, the transaction could not be agreed until $1 million could be found from someone who wished to make a deposit for the same term. Perfectly safe, but not many trades! Hard, though, to fault the logic. Indeed, the collapse of Bankhaus Herstatt a few years later showed how damaging the unexpected sum of a large number of individual deals could be, even though each transaction was made in perfect good faith. That is where the risk so often lies in devolved operations; not individual error, but the unlooked for coincidence that can cause catastrophe.

In a modern dealing room the scene is quite different. Each deal is recorded through key strokes on a terminal into the mainframe computer. The director can now see the net effect of all those individual transactions on the exposure of the bank, either in the particular currencies and securities, or over time. International banks can see their combined exposure across many dealing rooms around the world. If exposure is unattractive a minute after the London market closes, the risk can be offset in New York the following second. No more Herstatts now, except through deliberate judgement, or error at the highest level. And what of the effect on the dealers? They have been unleashed. Like lions, they can prowl the markets and snatch the deals, their leaders safe in immediate control of the sum of those individual activities. Organisation Man had to be harnessed tightly, because his freedom could spell disaster for the corporation; not so his successor.

The technology has had the same happy effect in the field of design. In a huge design project like System X, with its 2,500 engineers, or in the smallest team, computer aided design (CAD) makes possible the agreeable combination of maximum freedom for the individual designer, and preservation of those corporate benefits, like scale in purchasing components and standards for maintenance and testing. Armed with his screen, keyboard and mouse, the designer of a printed circuit board has a menu of permissible components that may be called up into the design. In devising that menu, senior management determines the variety of types it is prepared to buy. It can exclude components which may look attractive to the design engineer, but which are unsatisfactory commercially, if prone to faults in rough usage or to erratic supply. At least one small electronics company has failed to exert this control rigorously, and paid dearly when its well-conceived new terminal failed persistently during customer trials. Failures that eventually proved due to an integrated circuit intended for research use, and insufficiently robust for life in a typical office. The CAD system can also constrain the designer to avoid circuit patterns that risk electrical shorts, and layouts for inserted components that would be impractical for automatic machines. Again, many a small design team has found that its prototypes, that work so well in small numbers, are expensive to make, and desperately faulty when turned over to the large-scale production line, with its routine methods and automatic component insertion machines. All of these sad frustrations of talent can be avoided by taking advantage of the technology itself. A lesson that many small teams and new companies fail to learn, to their great cost.

What can be seen to apply so sharply in the special conditions of financial trading and in equipment design is equally relevant, if less obvious, in any organisation that has chosen to devolve power in response to competitive pressure and market turbulence. In every sort of organisation now, individuals must be encouraged to act with aggressive initiative to win their competitive battles – yet the criteria for prudence may not have changed at all. It is a bold and perhaps foolish chief executive who can devolve the power to make decisions, without at the same time putting in place a mechanism for understanding the sum of all those decisions on the crucial prudential factors. Banks need to know the net effect of thousands of decisions on their balance sheets, and on the pattern of risks to which they are exposed. Those factors are crucial to their prudent operation. Manufacturing companies need to know the sum effect of thousands of decisions in business units on common manufacturing facilities and on patterns of component and sub-system supply. Travel agents must not overbook – at least not too often. Insurance companies need to keep their portfolios of risks soundly balanced, while still offering the eager and instant service that today's customers expect. Hospitals have to manage the availability of beds and slots in theatre sessions; fire services may need to redeploy their engines, or call for help if fires break out all over. In all these varied areas of endeavour, in public service and in private, in manufacturing and in service businesses, the freedom for individuals to make their own decisions must be matched by appropriate systems to monitor the effect of all those decisions on the principal tasks of the enterprise, and above all on its survival.

DECIDING IN UNCERTAINTY

In one sense new technology can reduce uncertainty, in simulating the result of a complex series of events. Most dramatically, computers can generate holograms from all the data specifying the shape of an object – perhaps from a CAD system. But, in simpler image technology too, you can see what it looks like in three dimensions, without having to make it. More, you can change a parameter and watch the effect. The possibilities are rich; the biologist can picture a protein molecule, the architect could show his client the view across the entrance hall or from the boardroom door. The economics of a business can be modelled, and the effects of different decisions explored. For example, when BT first faced the competition of Mercury, a shadow team was set up to play out their possible strategies, allowing the responses to be tested – as the military play their war-games.

However, working in a turbulent world brings new risks. We see not just a plethora of new decision makers, but also individuals who have to make decisions on quite different criteria to those available in the long gone days of certainty. When BT's sixteen edge feet of Telecommunication Instructions could no longer be relied upon for perfect wisdom in every circumstance, people had to think for themselves! When regression analyses and extrapolations from the past are no longer safe guides to future actions, new clues are needed.

Individuals have to decide while uncertain; disconcerting for the accountants, so long used to evaluating projects with all those convincing cash flow forecasts and Net Present Value calculations! A favourite fallacy, so prevalent with Organisation Man and so unhelpful today, is the single line forecast. How often have we seen elaborate financial plans, stretching out a decade or more, based upon a single set of cost figures, a certain trend of annual revenues, and a launch date accurate to the month? What dangerous nonsense! Just occasionally, say when Rolls Royce was bankrupted by the RB 211 project at the end of the 1960s, a commercial event occurs that shocks managers for a year or two into doubting their certainties. Even engineers may wonder whether life is quite so predictable after all. Let their text be "Is it therefore infallibly agreeable to the Word of God, all that you say? I beseech you, in the bowels of Christ, think it possible you may be mistaken." Oliver Cromwell's words in August 1650 showed his anguish over the certainties of the Scottish kirk.

SAFETY NETS

I have always preferred to look at a profile of possible outturns before deciding on really major commitments. In a technique first developed in the 1960s while working in McKinsey's Chicago office

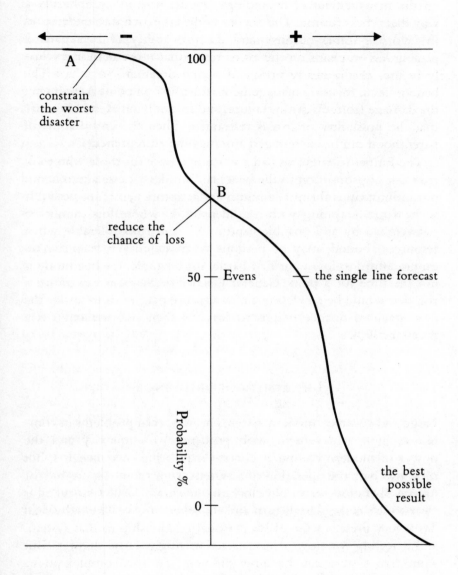

Figure 3 Manage risk to avoid catastrophe: Yield from an investment

on the management of technology, Figure 3 shows graphically a way that works for me. The essence of the approach is to understand the worst possible outturn, and the probability of breakeven – placing less emphasis on the evens result that most analysts exclusively use, or the heady prospects of the dreamer. So what? The benefit lies in focusing management effort first on point A, reducing the damage from disastrous failure, and secondly on B, making sure that the possibility of loss is restrained. Then the enthusiasms of parenthood can be encouraged amongst the entrepreneurs!

The Emperor Augustus had a word of advice for those who took risks out of proportion to the benefits: "similes ... esse aureo hamo piscantibus; cuius abrupti damnum nulla captura pensari posset" ("It is the same as fishing with a golden hook, whose loss cannot be outweighed by any possible capture").[1] And risks tolerable when resources abound, may be perilous when stability is fragile. You cannot afford to lose your first battle, for example; the beginning is not the time for a punt. General Electric or Siemens can afford a risk that would be reckless in a new venture that needs to justify the next stage of finance if it is to survive; then risk reduction is a necessary skill.

THE LIMITS OF PRUDENCE

Large and complex modern systems bring special problems in combining high achievement with prudence.[2] Complexity and the power of modern computer control may bring their benefits, but they also hide the operation of a system from those responsible for its safe operation. In an old clock, or in a traditional factory, all is clear to see as the wheels turn and the levers move. The individual has a very present sense of his personal relationship to that system, and a feeling for how a human action might cause disaster. But a modern system can be quite different; far too complex to be comprehended, controlled by intelligent boxes. The individual can soon feel personally irresponsible, because he cannot see the relationship between cause and effect. All too often, the computer's orders come with no explanation. If it tells you to press button A, press that button you must, abdicating responsibility because you have no way of knowing the quality of that instruction. It might derive from some algorithm based on an obsolete certainty, for example. What if some piece of equipment is shut down for maintenance, or a sensor is not working, or a new feedstock has been introduced? After all, systems may work well while circumstances remain predictable, but become turbulent if some new term becomes significant in the equation. To illustrate the point; while the line of performance is straight, one might assume that the governing equation was of the form $Y = MX + C$. But what if there is a term Z cubed? While Z is very small, the performance is just as predicted; but if Z becomes large, through some change in the system or the environment, events can become quite unexpected. Understanding the true nature of complex systems is a science, whose neglect lies behind many modern catastrophes.

In modern telecom systems, for example, computer-controlled exchanges operate well only within certain limits of traffic; then they are quite predictable, following the straight line of the simple equation. However, just like a roadway roundabout, they can become incapable of functioning at all, if those traffic limits are exceeded; the exchanges crash, in the jargon. If that characteristic is coupled with a large population of automatic dialling terminals, the conditions for a potential catastrophe have arrived. If, for example, a number of international circuits should be lost through an accident, the ruthless increase of repeat calls, as all those terminals hunt for a free line, could crash the international gateway. If that were to go, a major inland exchange could crash too, and so on through the network. A phenomenon nearly impossible with simple terminals, electromechanical exchanges, and human operators, is all too possible in the modern world. Capable of being managed, once recognised; a lurking disaster for the ignorant. In Britain and in the United States at least, new network management strategies should cope, but only because the unusual operation of the new system and the limits of performance were thought through.

Black Monday in August 1987 saw a similar, lemming-like behaviour within financial trading systems in New York. All those trading computers, set to sell automatically when stock prices moved below trigger levels, turned a downturn into a crash. We must all hope that regulators of trading systems since then will manage the instability of that particular factor, and bring back a bit more linearity to their world! Nuclear power stations, electric supply systems, chemical plants, offshore oil rigs, and modern transportation networks have all shown examples of systems that behave predictably until some new factor turns linear flow into turbulence. Understanding the true nature of complex systems, and conceiving the possible rogue factors that could disturb them, is a crucial feature of managing risk that has hitherto been neglected in many fields.

I disturbed a large gathering of safety specialists meeting in Washington in October 1988,[3] by suggesting that the traditional approach to risks that are not understood – applying ever larger safety factors – could make disaster more likely. Using the analogy of the skipper in a sailing boat seeking to win a race amongst the Greek Islands, I pointed out that an accurate chart was the only safe aid to victory with prudence. Since most industrial and commercial leaders are chosen for their urge to win, ignorance of where the rocks lie, masked by massive safety margins, is merely an incitement to play Russian roulette. With a good Admiralty chart, the skipper knows that he can sail within three metres of one cape, but thirteen would not be sufficient around another. Failing the chart, a rough rule of fifteen metres clear water around every cape would mean certain defeat; a cut corner could be catastrophic – but perhaps not. Which will the winner choose?

Fear of loss can debilitate. In a naval analogy, Lapeyrouse Bonfils, in his *Histoire de la Marine Française*,[4] had this to say about the poor showing of French fleets in the late eighteenth century in Admiral Mahan's translation:

Thanks to a wretched hesitation, fleets, which had rightly alarmed England, became reduced to ordinary proportions. Intrenching themselves in a false economy, the ministry claimed that, by reason of the excessive expenses necessary to maintain the fleet, the admirals must be ordered to maintain the "*greatest circumspection*", as though in war half measures have not always led to disasters ... a system which sapped moral power to save material resources ... It is certain that this deplorable system was one of the causes of the lack of discipline and startling defections which marked the periods of Louis XVI, and of the [first] Republic and of the [first] Empire.

Mahan's *The Influence of Sea Power upon History*,[5] transmitted that message to generations of naval officers, admiring Nelson's "No captain can do very wrong if he places his ship alongside that of an enemy." Admiral Halsey transformed the battle of Guadalcanal in two ferocious naval engagements, in which fine ships were lost, but the Japanese advance in the South Pacific was stopped dead. The British lost the battle of Gallipoli because the Navy would not run the risk of mines in the Dardanelles.

We must not debilitate our industrial leaders either. So we must learn more about where the edge of turbulence lies in modern systems if the new leaders are to welcome the scientific management of risk, rather than just pay lip service to an awkward social obligation. In the present fuzzy state of the art, how many chief executives really want to know about safety management – until after the fire or the explosion?

HUMAN FOIBLES

Catastrophes as varied as the release of methyl isocyanate at Bhopal, the radiation from Chernobyl, and the lethal fire in the Kings Cross underground station, London, were all made possible by weaknesses in physical systems, but were given their disastrous scale by fallacies in human ones. In Dr Bowonder's analysis for the World Bank, of the Bhopal disaster, for example, of some 126 causal factors, 93 can be attributed to the way in which people relate to the organisation and to each other; it was the cumulative effect of those failures, in regulation, in control systems, in values, and in management, that turned an incident into a catastrophe killing more than 2,000 people – and knocking one-third off Union Carbide's stock price. Intriguingly, Professor Rae Zimmerman[6] identifies some similar management and system failures contributing to the explosive release of aldicarb oxime, used with methyl isocyanate in making the pesticide Temik, nine months later in the same company's plant at Institute, West Virginia, injuring 135 people.

In the London subway catastrophe, it seems all too likely that management values were concerned more with minimising cost than with improving the quality of service or maintaining safety. In another British disaster, the release of radioactive material from

Britain's Sellafield site, one close observer finds causes in the preval-
ence of committees, and in slavish adherence to the rulebook,
which may be out of date. Committees allow their members to
share responsibility – syndicating risk – and that sharing can dilute
obligation.

Professor James Reason of Manchester University has used the
term "resident pathogens" to label the human factors that lie in wait
to cause major disasters out of minor mishaps.[7] Some types of
organisation, some management values and styles of leadership,
seem to nurture them; throwing money at the equipment may not
be the most effective way to make their systems safer. Look at the
Challenger disaster. Richard Feynman gives us an inside account of
the Presidential Commission.[8] That O-ring was classed among some
2,000 critical system factors, was known to operate imperfectly at
temperatures below 50°F, and the air temperature at launch was
below freezing, abnormally low for Florida – but the drive to meet
project timetables rode right over the engineers' warnings. That
being so, was it useful to spend a further $2 billion on enlarging the
safety envelope, or was the real need an improved sensitivity to
warning signals, and better communication throughout the project
leadership?

At that Washington conference in 1988 on preventing catastrophes, an eminent nuclear engineer gave his graphic view on the
mismatch in his industry between the enormous costs forced by
regulation on the designers, and what he saw as the inadequate
organisations that ran the plants day by day; "We hand those plants
over to animals", he told us. Hyperbole no doubt, but of a piece
with that sometimes excessive concern in the United States with
hardware, neglecting the human dimension – perhaps because it is
so difficult to measure and record to the satisfaction of the legalistic
regulator or the courts. Or are we perhaps observing in the United
States something of the separation of cultures so obvious in Britain?

American scientists and engineers can contribute their own professional disdain to the misunderstandings that damage the benefits
of so much advanced technology. At another conference a few
months later, I was astonished to hear an eminent US engineer
railing at the "scientific illiteracy" of senior government officials.
Speaking of the Star Wars program, he recited an anecdote about

the Secretary of Defense: "why, he didn't even know that an X-ray laser for space had to be pumped by an atomic bomb!" To which my response was to question whether any well-educated scientist – let alone layman – could reasonably be expected to know that esoteric fact, unless specialising in the area! As it happened, that particular Cabinet member had undoubtedly studied his science semesters at Harvard, and had recently spent six years as vice-president in an admirable high-technology engineering firm. So that outburst, which was greeted understandingly by other scientists present, seemed to show a general contempt for the so-called ignorance of able people not adept in a particular speciality, that must surely be ripe yeast for the bungling that creates catastrophes. No amount of dollars spent by the technologists in pursuit of infinite safety, or even inherent safety, as the meaningless phrase has it, is adequate compensation. Why, it even happens within the scientific community; until recently, science advisers to US Cabinet members used to send deputies to meetings chaired by the Science Adviser to the President!

The French have tackled their technology, and particularly their nuclear programme, rather differently and, it must be said, with considerably greater success. Their power plants are significantly cheaper than in the United States, but they have not yet suffered a catastrophe. Technical incidents and failures are regularly reported in the French press, but catastrophes do not follow. Why? An eminent French physicist, with a long career in academia, government, and industry, gave an explanation that convinced one Anglo-Saxon! He said:

All the leading figures involved in our nuclear industry come from the same intellectual background – the *hautes écoles*. People in government, the regulating department, the laboratories and the operators know and respect each other; they move among each other's organisations throughout their careers. And then, from the start we understood as a nation that we had to have nuclear power, even though it was not entirely without risk, because we would otherwise be quite without any significant national source of energy. We have taken the public into our confidence.

That account carries another important message: do not treat the public as we used to treat children, telling them fairy stories which must prove false. We all know of the shock when Father Christmas turns out to be Dad, but somehow trust is re-established in the family. Not so, when scientists lend their names to fairy-tale promises, or are brow-beaten by the lobbyists into silence on taboo topics! In the early 1970s there was a chance to come out; a Californian institute published a well-researched article calculating the number of avoidable deaths each year caused by two 1,000 megawatt power stations, one nuclear and the other coal fired. As I recall the figures, the coal plant was calculated to kill twelve each year, including miners with pneumoconiosis and people with diseases aggravated by sulphur dioxide and other pollutants. The figure for the nuclear plant was given as four. That was a reasonable comparison, and the calculations could have been tested in public debate, but the US nuclear industry preferred the pap of "inherent safety", and destroyed trust in their industry, and themselves.

THROUGH A GLASS DARKLY

Opacity in complex modern systems is a fruitful cause of disaster, fostering irresponsibility in those who cannot understand why their computers are telling them to act, nor what the consequences will be if they do so. A military analogy may help. Montgomery, commanding the Eighth Army in North Africa, used an unusual and very effective way of knowing what was going on that could hold a valuable lesson for the control of hazardous modern systems. As Nigel Hamilton tells us in *Monty, Master of the Battlefield*,[9] he sent quite junior officers right up to the front line, with radio sets capable of reaching directly to Army headquarters. That way Montgomery, or his chief of staff, knew up to the minute exactly what was going on in the turmoil of the front line – at least as far as anyone could tell. All those filtered reports coming up through the various levels of command, which were often so misleading and always delayed, could be read with an extra layer of significance: what intermediate commanders thought was happening, compared to the facts!

Now, electronic sensors are capable of measuring unobtrusively and accurately the state of any part of a system; pressure, rates of flow, nature of the traffic, temperature, the pace of change, and so on. But what to do with the information? Here is where the very latest advances in information technology can help. Driven first by the needs of military surveillance, artificial intelligence methods can replace the human brain in sorting out the significant, but a million times faster. The techniques that can track a submarine or help an admiral direct his carrier force efficiently in battle, could give the manager of a potentially catastrophic system the same sort of front-line view that Montgomery had in the desert through Captain Poston and his comrades. And if those intelligent systems were to expose to query the logic that leads them to advise particular actions, and the consequences of alternatives, then a sense of personal responsibility can return, displacing the blind, irresponsible faith in a dumb box.

Peter Kugler, in fascinating mathematical models of metastable systems, suggests that the onset of instability may be signalled by behaviour in the variables – notably by increasing amplitude of oscillations, and reduced frequency. Obviously valuable in handling aircraft at the limits of stability, could such phenomena perhaps make possible self-monitoring controls, capable of operating other systems safely at the limit of performance?

If modern complex and opaque systems are prone to catastrophe in the societies that develop them, might they be even more danger-ous if transplanted into foreign cultures? At that Washington con-ference, Professor Najmedin Meshkati of the University of Southern California was bold enough to break one of the unhelpful taboos that inhibit the discussion of ethnic characteristics, by asking whether the assembled experts on that October day in 1988 had considered what special problems might arise if the prevailing culture were to be fatalist. "What of Imshallah?", he enquired. Someone else pointed out that in a recent study of Chinese reactions to western danger signals, more than half had failed to recognise the red light as a warning. After all, red is the festival colour for Chinese, the emblem of joy.[10] Nearer home, a Yorkshireman is said to have followed his regional interpretation of the railway crossing sign "Wait while the lights are red", and was hit by the train. At present, complex systems in developing countries are usually run by men and women of the national elite, from leading families and educated in the world's finest colleges. Will similar systems be as safe when multiplied many times, in pursuit of nuclear power or advanced manufacture?

So, in the passing of Organisation Man, working within a stable structure in a stable and predictable environment, has come risk. Risk because the commercial environment has become turbulent; risk because decisions must now be passed from the inner group outwards to thousands of individuals; risk because modern systems are becoming larger, more complex, and more opaque; and finally, risk because modern technologies are so powerful, for good or ill, that their catastrophes become awesome. Understanding how to manage risk is crucial to survival and success in the modern world. The old techniques for mitigating risk – rigorous control and massive safety margins – are no answer in a fiercely competitive world. Those that follow such precepts will fail, and the bold will ignore them. Managing risk is a necessary new science – and it is not just for the technologists.

NOTES

1 C. Suetonius Tranquillus, *Opera Omnia* (Pralard, Paris, 1684), p. 129.
2 Rasmussen and others, *Safety Control and Risk Management*, ed. Rasmussen, Batstone (The World Bank, Washington, 1990).
3 Ibid.
4 Lapeyrouse Bonfils, *Histoire de la Marine Française*, vol. III (Dentu, Paris, 1845), p. 8.
5 A. T. Mahan, *The Influence of Sea Power upon History* (Sampson Low, Marston; London, 1890), p. 79.
6 Rae Zimmerman, "Understanding industrial accidents associated with new technologies", *Industrial Crisis Quarterly* (1988).
7 James Reason, "The contribution of latent human failures to the breakdown of complex systems", *Philosophic Transactions of the Royal Society* (1990).
8 Richard Feynman, *What do you Care what Other People Think?*, ed. R. Leighton (Bantam, New York, 1989).
9 Nigel Hamilton, *Monty, Master of the Battlefield* (Hamish Hamilton, London, 1983), p. 762.
10 C. A. S. Williams, *Outlines of Chinese Symbolism and Art Motives* (Kelly and Walsh, Shanghai, 1932), p. 75.

PART V

CAN IT LAST?

Limits to growth recede as the service economy proves itself. Real jobs and real wealth, even though the products break no bones.

The enterprise culture reaches the third world, stirring renewed strengths in old trading societies, now that communication networks bring capability to all.

Another paradox: where high technology permeates, people matter. The humane society is back, now the silicon chip is anyone's helot. It pays to be decent, honest and frank, because no man is an island.

A prosperous and happy world can be, but fragility threatens; let obligations weigh more than rights. Different solutions for the varied cultures of mankind, but for the human spirit, newly freed: there's the chance – go for it!

II

WHERE WILL THE JOBS COME FROM?

Dooms deflected

At the end of the nineteenth century, the British Association for the Advancement of Science made headlines with projections that the world would inevitably run out of food for its increasing population. While in Ethiopia and the Sudan, in their special climatic conditions, that worry is proving justified, no one predicted that Europe could be in such massive surplus. For the developed countries at least, human ingenuity has held at bay the dire predictions of Malthus and those Victorian scientists. Professor Golden did refer to the issue in a lecture to the American Association for the Advancement of Science in 1989, but among twenty-one other problems, under the cheerful title "Cheer up, things could be worse".

Between those two eminent gatherings, in a predominantly manufacturing economy the Club of Rome predicted that many of the world's crucial raw materials would be completely exhausted within a century. As recently as 1972, their report, *The Limits To Growth*,[1] proposed a new doom – a world in which growth in developed economies and emergence of the third world would be quite incompatible.

Now we can see that neither the shortage of food, nor the shortage of raw materials is likely to be an imminent threat to the expansion of prosperity throughout the world. Other factors may well disrupt the process, but not those ones. Human ingenuity, and the operation of the market place have expanded supply, and shown how we can use scarce resources to better effect. Now a new doom is threatened. People locked in the concepts of the manufacturing age predict that, even though output may continue to grow, employment will fall and fall dramatically. Sober forecasts in the United States predict less than 10 per cent of the workforce will be engaged in making things by the year 2000, and some doubt whether an economy is sustainable on such narrow employment in producing real things. Could these new doomsters be wrong too?

THE NEW WEALTH

The service economy which now provides two-thirds of jobs in Britain, and rather more in the United States, has its worried critics, for all its obvious economic significance. With suggestions that real wealth comes from manufacturing, and that prosperity in the service economies is little more than washing each other's motor cars, we are watching once again a clash of cultures. Rather reminiscent in its way of the conflict between classical learning and the modern, played with by Jonathan Swift in *An Account of a Battel between the Ancient and Modern Books in St James's Library*.[2] Set in the King's library, the modern volumes contend for the highest peak in Parnassus. The battle is joined after old Aesop suggests derisively that the spider should be the symbol of the moderns: "Erect your Schemes with as much Method and Skill as you please; yet if the Materials be ... spun out of your own Entrails ... the Edifice will conclude at last in a *Cobweb*." While the bee, representing the ancients, produced real wealth,

Whatever we have got, has been by infinite Labour and Search, and ranging through every corner of Nature. The Difference is, that instead of *Dirt* and *Poison*, we have rather chose to fill our Hives with *Honey* and *Wax*; thus furnishing Mankind with the two Noblest of Things, which are, *Sweetness* and *Light*.

Well, quite a lot of manufacturers feel in their bones that the service economy too is a huge cobweb, but are they right?

The fallacy seems to lie in regarding manufacturing and service activities as lying in two separate economies, when of course they are just aspects of the same phenomenon. They are both concerned with creating wealth, through adding value for the consumer. Certainly, now that customers have choice, the manufacturer who believes that the service economy is for others is turning his back on opportunities for adding value, and perhaps on his market place itself. For the successful manufacturer, service is built into the product through good design; supports the product into the market place through good distribution; extends its life and usefulness through good maintenance; and perhaps the product itself can be a vehicle for launching further services.

Indeed, the added value perceived by the customer in the services may be many times greater than the plain cost of the unvarnished hardware itself. Sometimes that further value is added by the manufacturer; more often by others who have spotted an opportunity to extend by another link the chain of processes stretching from the original sand of the silicon circuit, or the iron ore of the machine tool. But whoever adds that extra value – if it is perceived as such by a customer – creates wealth. The hardware is of course usually necessary for the services, but if the global market is working well, that will be obtainable. Facilitating standards in computing like OSI, give downstream providers an entry into IBM systems; legislation gave film processors the chance to compete on level terms with Kodak.

THE VALUE CHAIN

But manufacturers do have a flying start in seizing service added value, with all its benefits. Digital has shown how one manufacturer can double its annual growth in profits through moving firmly downstream from its hardware product base towards the services that every computer customer needs. IBM, with its tremendously strong customer relations, has found an additional virtue. Whenever its product development has faltered, or a competitor has leapt in with a new concept – like the personal computer – those strong customer loyalties have acted like a flywheel in an engine, giving it time to react and to correct. In the same industry, Canada's Mitel stands as a warning of how quickly a manufacturer with weak service links to its customers can collapse. Founded by two young English immigrants to Toronto, Mitel succeeded brilliantly while its research and development programmes successively produced excellent products on time. Sadly, though, when the really big one came along – the SX 2000 digital PABX – the run of good luck ended. Mitel just could not get the software to work well, and the SX 2000 missed its technological window; the company was lucky to be rescued by BT.

What went wrong? After all, when IBM failed to develop a successor to its 3750 PABX, it stayed in the market and was able to turn for a replacement first to Mitel, and then to Rolm when Mitel failed to track down its software bugs. Mitel's problem was that it had negligible links to the final customer. As Terry Mathews, Mitel's chairman, explained to me back in 1980, his corporate strategy was to reach the market through distributors rather than a direct sales force. That certainly meant good new products could achieve wide success quickly; but there was no ratchet. Distributors are fickle, certainly if they fear their markets will disappear unless they can find a new supplier to replace the troubled product. Mitel's distributors deserted in droves when it was clear that the new PABX was in deep trouble, as they had to if they were to survive themselves. In Britain, Norton Telecommunications switched to Siemens; in the United States, Mitel plummeted from number two position to an also-ran in a few months. All the more surprising that BT should have paid so much for such a fragile route into the American market!

There is a valuable lesson in Mitel's cautionary tale for every new venture in a high technology industry. With product lives as short as three or four years, it is simply imprudent to rely just on scientific muscle to produce successive generations of new products ahead of competitors each time, with trouble-free launch. Those that provide the money, the venture capitalists, want to build businesses, not just launch clever, once in a lifetime products. They reap their harvest when a new company can be floated on the stock market – and that needs a steady record of financial performance. Where the technology develops rapidly, the company's flotation might well be in the third technical generation; so building customer loyalties, to give trading continuity through technical difficulties, makes good financial sense for the investor and for the entrepreneur. Incidentally, since it is quite unpleasant to fall into a profit pit after your shares have reached the public domain, the benefits of customer loyalty, once earned, will not lose their charm!

END OR BEGINNING?

The manufacturing and mechanical frame of mind can be very resistant to the new opportunities in adding wealth through service. In BT the PABX was for years seen as the end of the network, rather than as a bridgehead into the rich pastures of the service economy in all those millions of customer organisations. Hence that costly error in giving local telecom areas not just the responsibility for selling advanced equipment, but even the freedom to select and purchase their products idiosyncratically. That distracted local management from providing good quality service to monopoly customers, and impaired for years the expansion of BT from its own network into the rich added value waiting to be harvested in customer systems.

US West, based in Denver, learnt the lesson a little quicker under their chairman, Jack McAllister, and set up new business divisions to exploit the new opportunities. They reaped two harvests; good local service to the ordinary telephone user, and new businesses capable of providing long-term growth. The regulated monopoly businesses were run well according to their own criteria, satisfying the domestic customer with his crucial influence on the rate-setting process; the fiercely competitive business systems market needed a quite different sort of style – and the management values that could deliver it. So service businesses need to be organised to match the market, not the old corporate baronies.

WHOSE VALUES?

Even in traditional manufacturing, neglect of service can destroy profits. In my first engineering company, we could not sell successfully to the process plant industry in Europe, against a straight copyist of our product pricing 10 per cent higher. Why? Because our delivery was unreliable, causing penalty payments by our contractor customers. One even suggested that he could not afford our valves even if they were free. And that beautifully designed air conditioning plant did not sell in the Persian Gulf, because it was not designed for easy maintenance and repair. The Volkswagen first triumphed in the United States because its repair and service organisation was exemplary. In the same market, whenever two or three Jaguar owners were gathered together, they capped each other's horror stories about unreliability and poor service; and so an admired product was regarded as hopelessly impractical for all but the mechanically minded, the philosophical, and those hardy souls who cherish rarity.

There really can be no argument on the matter; manufacturing is within the service economy, and not separate from it. As Kazuyoshi Ishizaka of Japan's Kenwood Corporation put it to Stanford Design Forum in 1988, intangible, unmeasurable and subjective factors count.

BY SERVICE ALONE?

And what of service businesses themselves? If they are to be important in our lives, creating jobs and wealth, do they need a healthy manufacturing sector for their own prosperity? One argument holds that a free market will see that every need is met; whatever equipment a service business may need will surely be available, if it can be produced anywhere. But how efficient are markets? Certainly we see in technology important for defence, significant barriers to its availability, where ideas might leak through to a potential enemy. COCOM, the agency by which America's allies control the flow of advanced technology, has tried very hard to prevent advanced information technology reaching the Soviet bloc. So far, the market for equipment seems to work well for British customers; but if West German firms can fall under some suspicion, how reliable are those market forces for the rest of Europe? If senators are concerned today about the flow of hard technology, what will they and their colleagues feel about software tomorrow, which can move so inconspicuously across national frontiers? And then, even should defence issues not arise, can one advanced economy really rely on a competitor to hasten the flow of new hardware if it can crucially affect the success of a major service industry? Even the United States, an exemplar of open markets, sees its government quite willing to issue commercial fiats in the interest of foreign or trade policy;

observe the constraints on open market operations, to protect the optronics and semi-conductor industries, or to force reciprocity from Japan.

It does seem prudent, therefore, that governments in complex economies should encourage the development of crucial enabling technologies within their borders, or at least make sure they keep some irresistible influence over potential suppliers. Is it perhaps negligent for a government to reject the concept of a national strategy in technology or commerce when that rejection is based on the expectation of a perfect market? Imperfections in the real market may be noticed too late, unless crucial capabilities have been preserved through special measures. Mind you, crass protectionism will not work either, if it shelters too safely a home industry from the best developments elsewhere in the world. Getting that balance right needs a phrase or two in a national strategy as well. As with lesser organisations, governments can err either in controlling too rigidly, or in abdicating entirely. A light framework of strategy and structure to preserve the essentials, leaving the entrepreneurs to create the initiatives, works well in business. It should work for nations as well; it certainly does for Japan!

However important the service economy may be for our futures, much of the infrastructure to commerce is still organised for manufacturing industry. Balance sheets record physical assets, but not the software in information systems; they often ignore the intellectual property in technology or in reputation and brand names. Where goodwill is given a value, it is just a euphemism for having paid more for a company than the shareholders' net worth shown in the accounts. A disinclination among accountants and analysts to recognise the economic value of an asset that cannot be counted in a stock check, but yet is capable of creating wealth, inhibits businesses from building their service strengths. After all, if a business in high technology needs to spend, say, 8 per cent of sales each year on research and development, as much on strategic information systems and huge sums in training and setting up international distribution systems, any reluctance among investors to count those new capabilities in the value of the company can discourage the building of necessary competitive power. One argument of the financiers is that if the expenditures have been well judged, then the wealth will be generated in due course and the stock price will reflect that new prosperity. But what if a predator moves first?

TOWARDS AN ENTERPRISE CULTURE

If the service economy in its many forms is crucial to the creation of jobs and wealth, so too is the small business. Professor David Birch of MIT has for a decade now been charting just where the new jobs are created in the United States.[3] Drawing on the Dunn and Bradstreet database, which covers some 80 per cent of private sector employment, he makes some intriguing observations. First, that throughout the United States, the rate of job loss through obsolescence and improvement in productivity is remarkably constant: around 8 per cent each year in communities across the land. The difference between full employment and unemployment lies not in the rate of job loss, but in job creation. Secondly, he observes that 80 per cent of new jobs are created in companies employing fewer than 100 people, two-thirds come from those with fewer than twenty employees; the Fortune 500 giants have shed labour massively over the last two decades. If that experience is valid elsewhere, though not yet measured, it certainly implies that in the service era we need an effective enterprise culture too, if the massive improvement in manufacturing productivity is not to create unemployment, with all its social strains and wasted opportunity.

But what makes for an enterprise culture? Why does it work so well along Route 128 around Boston, but not in Ulster or Bavaria? Perhaps we are seeing again the phenomenon that Sismondi[4] observed to be at work in those trade guilds of master craftsmen and traders in the cities of north Italy, 500 years ago and more. Once people feel capable of prospering on their own, without the protective strength of the Organisation, then freedom flourishes, and the individual strikes out on his own. For that confidence, it certainly helps to have seen how a business ticks.

David Fell, Permanent Secretary of the Northern Ireland Department of Economic Development, wrote a thoughtful paper in 1986, identifying two particular problems in that economy, which may be of wider concern. First, the massive influence of state employment and purchasing has created a sense of dependence rather than initiative. Secondly, that for all too many of those who did work in the trading sector, the employer was just a functional unit, controlled in detail from abroad, by an owner attracted to Ulster by generous government grants and allowances. American Brand's Gallaher cigarette and tobacco factories and STC's assembly plant for electronic equipment are examples among many. So, Fell's argument runs, there are just too few individuals with both the spirit and the experience to launch new businesses, and to make them prosper.

Scotland too has been successful in landing manufacturing investment by multinationals; but 90 per cent of workers in the electronics industry work for companies managed from outside the country. Tax havens have a similar problem; the island of Jersey, for example, may have been highly successful in attracting offshore financial institutions, but what work do they give their people to do? It seems that a temporary prosperity may be destroying the seeds of an enterprise culture there; local businesses are disrupted, their people drawn away to do routine, if well paid, clerical jobs. Does it not seem that attracting inward investment may be like taking a stiff drink: immediate pleasure, followed by a headache? Can that sort of government policy augur well for an enterprise culture? What if conditions change, say low tax rates in financial centres, or higher bids from a competitor nation? Perhaps the answer lies in requiring a degree of autonomy for local management; prefer the self-standing businesses; investment management rather than offshore transaction shops, for example. Of course, operating subsidiaries of transnational groups can make a marked contribution to entrepreneurial capability, developing exceptional business leaders, and be venturesome to boot. Texas Instruments, IBM, and Ford have all launched individuals who have left the parent and built indigenous businesses outside the United States, and Heinz found their group CEO in Ireland; the Japanese have not, so far.

Germany seems to face rather different problems in stimulating entrepreneurs. No shortage of successful and powerful German companies, but still a weak venture industry. Why should that be? Perhaps Germany, for all its industrial strength, has persisted too long in sheltering its industries from international competition. The Bundespost is a byword for protectionist control in telecommunications, imposing an impregnable buy-German policy. In other sectors, the German economy seems still to encourage cartel-like behaviour banished in the United States and Britain. So, since the conditions for Organisation Man still persist, it is not so surprising that functional organisations with rigid specialisms persist in Germany more virulently than a free market would allow. Some venture capitalists and management consultants who can compare across Europe's borders, confirm that in Germany general managers are hard to find. Perhaps that is why Siemens invest such substantial funds in British ventures. A successful enterprise culture surely needs an abundant supply of general management talent, people with zest but also the ability to co-ordinate all the functions in the creation of wealth. If that is necessary to the large company, it is vital to the small team. We need general managers to create new jobs and full employment.

But such blemishes in the tilth of western enterprise cultures are as nothing to the condition of Eastern Europe. Seeds of new initiative find the stoniest ground in the communities newly emerging from the paralysing bureaucracy of communist central planning. If Ulster's economy can be described as dependent, a very much stronger adjective is needed for the environment of Poland, Hungary, Rumania, or Czechoslovakia. Forty years of scarcity and byzantine regulations have sapped the creativity of all but the most resilient; specialisation has been carried right up to the State Planning and the Foreign Trade Commissions – and indeed back to the economic planners of COMECON. *Perestroika* needs a helping hand from the West, if freedom is to produce the fruits of individual initiative before the creaking state systems crack apart. Liberty may lose some of its charm, if scarcity and poverty seem to flow from it.

FOOD FOR THE MIND

We need creativity too, and that can be worked for as well. As Poincaré pointed out,[5] one good step is to stock minds well with the facts and concepts that can form the raw material for an idea out of the rut. The subconscious is capable of marvellous things, but it helps to give it matter to feed on; as the midwife mother of Socrates said, "the baby must be there, if it is to be delivered"! Edward de Bono suggests another requirement too.[6] The orthogonal approach; seeing an old situation from a fresh viewpoint. One of de Bono's French disciples built a nice little consulting practice leading teams towards a new-found creativity, with an unusual variant. "Imagine you are a bird," he used to say, "fly over your problem and see if it looks different that way!" Well, that may work for some, but easier advice might be to imagine yourself just as your own customer. So easily seductive to move along the tramlines of development, the family tree – son, grandson and great grandson – of the original successful idea. In my mechanical valve company in the 1970s, the designers' next generation of product always had those uncanny family resemblances – father's nose and mother's chin! Not least of the benefits from taking value in the customer's eyes as a guide lies in the spark to creativity that an unfamiliar viewpoint can strike.

PROSPERITY FOR ALL?

So prospering in the new economy, in which service pervades, does not call just for the sharpest intellects and the broadest conceptual powers; it also needs the human qualities of curiosity, sympathy, and the ability to think afresh. Wherever those qualities can be found, the new prosperity can follow, and not only in the advanced economies.

In the developing countries, the power of telecommunications to transform societies has been clearly shown. First, the great trading centres like Singapore and Hong Kong, that depend on networks as good as any in the world, but then also the larger, rural populations, like Malaysia and Brazil. Economies that harvested commodities and let the world's middlemen take the rest of the added value, find themselves able to reap more from what they have sown. Economic studies in the Nile Delta and in Kenya show how soon service industries can spring up in agricultural communities, once telecommunication links are established with the rest of the world.

Many so-called developing countries have a venturing history, leaving latent characteristics in their people, now emerging. For centuries the communities bordering the Indian Ocean and the China Seas have traded ambitiously: Canton, Hanoi, Bangkok, Malacca, Batavia, Madras, Goa, Muscat, Basra, Jedda, Cairo, and Aleppo were all great merchant centres before the first Englishman landed on the shores of the James river. With political freedom, information technology and its powerful new international networks offer the first major opportunity in two centuries for those traditional skills to burgeon. The new technology's harvest does not depend on an advanced local technical base, but on the creative use of the new capabilities – and that fecundity of invention may well lie latent in populations that have shown an adventurous trading spirit in their untrammelled past.

In those circumstances, governments that direct their policies to nurturing local advanced technology may have got their priorities wrong. The wealth that information technology makes possible for them is many times greater than earnings from the technology itself. It is inconceivable that any science that an international company is prepared to transfer to a developing nation would not be freely available on the world market, should the need for alternative supply arise. So artificial protection of home manufacturers may not make economic sense in China, Malaysia or elsewhere, if it hampers their entrepreneurs in reaching the services and systems they need for their own commercial success.

As more of the rather special skills of the software specialists become embedded in the increasingly intelligent equipment, the scope for imaginative and sympathetic human beings to prosper through advanced technology will grow. When motor cars were first seen, they were driven by specially trained chauffeurs. When computers first appeared, their mysteries were tended by a breed apart. The motor car has become a commonplace for everyone; the computer, with all its power to create wealth as an aid to human initiative, is for Everyman too. The most dramatic benefits are already coming to those with the imagination to use the new capabilities – not just to those able to create them. After all, who really harvested the wealth made possible by the motor car? Henry Ford and his workers, or the travel industry, owners of property, and the oil companies? The high technology age, and the service economy, is for everyone.

PEOPLE, TOO PRECIOUS TO SQUANDER

Indeed, so successful has the service economy been where free to develop, that a new concern is looming. First in those offshore communities like Jersey and Guernsey, and now in the prosperous regions of southern Britain, Massachusetts, and California, there is a nascent recognition that economic growth may be limited by the availability of people, particularly those with useful skills. With a 30 per cent reduction in twenty-year-olds just a few years away in some countries, official policies of job creation – any jobs – begin to look misguided. Except for the few areas where the collapse of a massive local industry has removed jobs faster than enterprise can create them, the task now is surely to promote added value; if people are a scarce resource, then economic sense lies in helping each individual to create the maximum wealth of which he or she may be capable. It is economic sense also to attract people into the workforce, making it easier for women – and indeed the disabled – to add value in a way that is feasible for their circumstances.

Provided, then, that the world's economic framework continues to foster free trade and open markets, the prospects for employment in the "post industrial era" look remarkably promising. In the new service economies of the West the old alarms of shortages of energy and materials seem to have receded; when wealth is represented not so much by physical assets as by the fruit of human ingenuity or of human service, the limits to growth postulated by the Club of Rome are of doubtful relevance. Pollution could make the new prosperity disagreeable and dangerous; catastrophic failure of large man-made systems is an ever-growing threat, witness Chernobyl and the Sandoz contamination of the Rhine; a major discontinuity in oil prices could destabilise dependent developing economies, since western banks are unlikely to play the recycling role again after their horror of non-performing third-world debt; war, and its interruption of the pyramid of mutual benefit from international trade, could bring the whole happy process to an inglorious end.

But with those spectres exorcised, the processes at work now promise increasing wealth of a rather civilised nature in the advanced economies, and a prospect that traditional skills, so widely latent in the third world, will bring their nations greater prosperity too. Banishing those spectres is a major responsibility for statesmen.

NOTES

1 Cole, Freeman, Jahoda and Pavitt (eds), *Thinking about the Future, a Critique of the Limits to Growth* (Chatto & Windus, London, 1973), pp. 14–32, 132–4.
2 Jonathan Swift, *An Account of a Battel between the Ancient and Modern Books in St James's Library* (Nutt, London, 1704), pp. 249–51.
3 David L. Birch, *The Job Generation Process*, (MIT, Cambridge, Mass., 1979), p. 21.
4 J. C. L. Sismondi, *History of the Italian Republics*, ed. W. Boulting (Routledge, London, n.d.), p. 159.
5 Henri Poincaré, *Science et Méthode* (Flammarion, Paris, 1908).
6 Edward de Bono, *Lateral Thinking* (Ward Lock, London, 1970).

12

THE HUMANE SOCIETY

AD UNGUEM FACTUS HOMO

So, as advanced technology permeates every aspect of our lives, the humane skills become more important; the fully-formed individual, in Horace's phrase, comes into his own. Just as Correlli Barnett and others seem to be winning in their assault on liberal education, maybe those arts of human relationships are once again indispensable. After all, if understanding the customer's perception of value is the best way of judging what he is going to buy, it helps to see things his way. If running a modern organisation well means giving a lot of people the freedom to act, then the art of inspiring initiative in others may be rather valuable. If a collegiate sentiment will get the best out of whoever can give the bright ideas, then a sympathetic style may work better than the flat instruction or abrupt demand. When a fruitful relationship in a new market depends on a feeling for the prejudices and enthusiasms one might expect to find, then history and literature may not seem so remote from commerce. All rather different to the world of scarcity and the mechanical economy.

In my first engineering company, back in the early 1970s, the export department was just one man and some typists. There he sat, surrounded with customs documents from fifty countries, shipping schedules, and files of correspondence with distributors. Those were the days when foreign contacts visited the factory once a year, and expected a return visit from the chairman in his Bentley on a leisurely continental tour. Rather a different emphasis; it was the Works that counted in those days of scarcity, making things and getting them out of the door. A mechanical age, when specialists dealt with functionaries in structures, rather than colleagues. Why, in my five years or so at BT I can scarcely recall being addressed by my name – always the initials of my position, MDT or DC! – but perhaps that was exceptional.

And now we have service economies. If fewer than 10 per cent of the workforce is going to be involved in actually making objects with machines inside factories, then most of us will be concerned in our working lives with that very human activity, serving other people. To do that well requires developed human qualities; ingenuity and creativity yes, but also a desire to understand how other people relate to their own circumstances, and what they value. With the clever and complex technology now more and more hidden behind a friendly computer screen and a standard terminal, it is no longer necessary to understand the technology in detail in order to use it fruitfully. Of course, we are all dependent on well-trained and inventive scientists for the improved tools, and certainly we need to understand what those tools are capable of, but for most the rich harvest comes from devising the application and not engineering the technology itself. Thirty years ago the situation was quite different. Then we were in a mechanical age, in which the flexibility of technology was relatively limited and understanding its limitations was crucial to commercial success. In most industries, the product offered to the customer was constrained by the technology rather than the imagination of the user. But that has changed. I recall a visit to the IBM research labs at Hursley, in southern England; John Fairclough remarked, "something seemed to change in the mid-seventies; before then it was the quality of your R & D team that made all the difference, but now it's whether your kit is easy for the customer that counts." Now the technology is so powerful that even last year's marvel is quite enough for most of us. Just make it simple to use, is the plea.

So Correlli Barnett in *The Audit of War*,[1] has been quite right to castigate an education system that gave Britain's leaders before 1945 so little understanding of the technology on which the industrial revolution, and international trade, depended. He was right on that theme to quote Herbert Spencer, who wrote in 1861:

and here we see most distinctly the vice of our educational system ... it neglects the plant for the sake of the flower. In anxiety for elegance, it forgets substance. While it gives no knowledge conducive to self-preservation – while of knowledge that facilitates gaining a livelihood it gives but the rudiments, and leaves the greater part to be picked up any how in afterlife ... it is diligent in teaching whatever adds to refinement, polish, eclat.

But is it helpful today to imply that the philistine will inherit the earth?

Narrow liberals

Barnett seems to be broadening, though. Writing in 1989, he looks for the humanities to develop from a too exclusively literary approach that prizes the critical and analytical skills above practical creativity and problem solving. That reflection has been justified for three centuries, echoing as it does Jonathan Swift's metaphor,[2]

for, pray Gentlemen, was anything so *Modern* as the *Spider*, in his Air, his Turns, and his Paradoxes? ... that he Spins and Spits wholly from Himself and scorns to own any Obligation or Assistance from Without.

In 1697 as in 1897, classical scholarship was still concerned substantially with the fine tuning of the classical texts, and tightly argued criticisms of particular points in logic or theology. Earlier, Erasmus launched the charge of obscurantism at the scholastics of the Middle Ages, and indeed of his own time, enemies of enlightenment. Famous disputes on how many angels could dance on the head of a pin, and the like, did little to endear theology to the man in the street, though no doubt highly stimulating for those in the game. While we must be grateful to Richard Bentley for the knowledge that the lover in Horace's ode attacked his girlfriend's door with axes not with bows,[3] and for many other emendations to faulty manuscripts, Swift implied that the contribution of Horace was far greater than that of the textual critic. Of course Swift had some animus in the case, since Bentley had just attacked successfully his patron Sir William Temple, who had mistakenly praised a spurious Latin text.

WHAT IS ROME TO US?

So, perhaps the lesson for us is to encourage young people to see past the syntax and grammar of the classical languages into the extraordinary works that have been preserved from antiquity, with their observations on how men and women relate to each other in conditions often as turbulent as our own, or more so. While Latin, for example, has its particular merits as a language – concise and capable of great variety in rhythm and sound – it is surely the ideas and human relationships described, in the tiny body of classical works that survives, that can bring most to the modern individual seeking to prosper in a turbulent age.

Saint Augustine's "I know because we measure ... but what may be measured will not be"[4] seems to me a truly significant concept, distilled by a great mind ruminating in a deeply disrupted society. The personal philosophy of Augustus, one of history's most successful leaders, is surely valuable today? The metaphor of the golden fishhook, whose loss could not be compensated by any conceivable catch, is too valuable an idea to disappear from our minds. The Roman admiration for Fabius Cunctator, who wore out Hannibal's strength through indecisive battles, could be valuable to a hothead today, faced with an opponent too strong to be engaged in flat out contest. "Unus homo nobis cunctando restituit rem" ("one man through delay gave us back our power") might well have inspired Marshal Kutuzoff's campaign against Napoleon after Borodino, and Stalin's against Hitler. I certainly found it a helpful concept in wresting power from BT's unions at the end of the 1970s. A head-on attack then could have been just as disastrous as the reckless Roman assault on Hannibal at Cannae, which made Fabius' cautious policy so respectable.

And are there no lessons to be learnt from Cicero's magical command of even a hostile audience? The generation of Pitt and Burke had Blair's *Lectures*;[5] in our time Edward Corbett, of Ohio State University, wrote a most instructive book, *Classical Rhetoric for the Modern Student*,[6] with illustrations from Ronald Dworkin, Malcolm X, John F. Kennedy, James Baldwin, Martin Luther King, and others, whose skilful use of language influenced so remarkably the minds of men and women in the 1960s. Virgil was inspired by

Homer; intriguing to see Odysseus' plea to Achilles in the *Iliad*, compared to arguments persuading the reluctant Eisenhower or Stevenson to run for President.

By Cicero's time, several hundred years of practical experience had fashioned a structure in presenting an argument that might well be valuable today – it has certainly worked for some very successful persuaders over the past 2,000 years. Exordium, Narration, Partition, Confirmation, Refutation, and Peroration. An introduction to describe the objective of the discourse and to settle the audience into a receptive mood. Then a review of the facts, organising the presentation, followed by a defence of the preferred proposition, confirming its merits. Next, having established a grasp of the situation and a positive attitude towards finding solutions, comes the refutation of the opposing point of view, either by reason, by appeals to the emotions or to ethics, or by wit and ridicule. Even there the classics can help; Quintilian on oratory said "there are no jests so insipid as those which parade the fact that they are intended to be witty." And then the conclusion, recapitulating the arguments and forming the final state of mind of the audience.

Erasmus used just that structure in his *The Praise of Folly*, as Professor Hudson of Princeton has shown.[7] I followed Hudson's analysis in the Harvard Club library, writing my speech to defend the contentious statement "there shall be a licence to manage", at the 1989 World Management Congress, in New York City; at least they listened, and one New Yorker slipped me a note, "you *are* on the right track". Dworkin used a similar arrangement in *Not prosecuting civil disobedience*, as Professor Corbett describes. How many business propositions would have succeeded if they also had been presented with techniques that have proved effective in so many various human situations?

Cicero believed too that the rhythm and spacing of sounds could deeply influence people. In his book *Orator*, addressed to Marcus Brutus, who plunged the last dagger into Julius Caesar, he gave an illustration from the speech of an opponent.[8] He claimed that the ending caused tremendous clamour and excitement: "patris dictum sapiens, temeritas filii comprobavit". A cretic, long syllable short long, followed by two trochees, each a long and a short, caused the effect, in Cicero's view. The words mean "the rashness of the son confirmed the wisdom of the father"; Cicero suggests to Brutus that the same sense but with a different sequence of sounds would have fallen quite flat. "Try this, comprobavit filii temeritas: it is nothing at all."

Dr Thaddaeus Zielinski, of pre-revolutionary St Petersburg, found that every one of Cicero's speeches ended in the same way: a cretic followed by two trochees, or a metrical equivalent. Is that information quite useless today? Was the Roman ear so different from ours that metre in prose is insignificant? I hardly think so. The Fellows of the Institute of Public Relations reacted rather well in 1989 to the clausula "Understand and be understood, that's the ticket"; a conference on Telecommunication Policy seemed warmed by "ISDN, there's the key: seize it; use it"; the chief fire officers applauded "In turbulent times, every established system has a fallacy; understand where it's lurking." Not quite Cicero's "Hoc dichoreo tantus clamor concionis excitatus est, ut admirabile esset" ("with this double trochee there was a wonderful clamour in the audience"), but then, as he wrote to Brutus, "In praestantibus rebus, magna sunt ea, quae sunt optimis proxima." ("In great matters, even those that approach the best are great"!) Reminiscent of that Boston story of the two MBA's, Harvard and MIT perhaps, meeting a bear when out back-packing. One unpacks his running shoes; "Why bother, you'll never run fast enough to escape that bear?"; "Ah! But I'll run faster than you!" You do not need to be perfect, just better than the other guy.

If classical literature is read, not as an exercise in linguistics, but for the rich portrayal of concepts and values in human relationships, then those works must be of very great significance to an individual in the new humane society of the service economy. In that small body of classical literature, with the best ideas from inventive Greece distilled through the firm characters and practical minds of Rome, these works have much to teach us. That they have survived only through being copied and copied again repeatedly throughout the centuries, has winnowed away the dross; what remains for us has proved its relevance in every variety of the human situation. So after all, in the modern call for education for capability, if the defenders of the humanities can draw that practical modern value from their subjects, then they too fall within the circle of the blessed. Up to them, really.

CITIZENS OF THE WORLD

How else are we to develop those qualities of curiosity, sympathy and sensitivity that seem so important in a turbulent market place, abundant with choice? Certainly an export strategy that fails to understand the distinctive culture and desires in different communities will fail. Marks and Spencer, so successful at retailing in Britain, scarcely shone at first in Paris, except for those Frenchmen who smoke English cigarettes. A proposition that sells admirably to the practical British, seeking their "good sensible underclothes", may look unexciting where flair and novelty carry greater weight in the prevailing value system.

An Italian once described to me the marketing strategy for Fernet Branca, as hitting the repentance market. After an indulgent dinner that bitter liquor, tasting like grandmother's stomach medicine, seems just the thing to express modified contrition. Would that platform work in Washington? And what of that eminent Genovese who carried in his mental infrastructure 600 years of his city-state, artful against invasive powers? And the influence of Napoleon on French government and education; can we judge a Frenchman's preferences unless we can distinguish between a Parisian *fonctionnaire* and a person of good family in the Vendée, royalist still? And who makes the financial decisions in a French family business? Rather different to the world of Alf Garnett or Archie Bunker. No, in a turbulent world, global for those who can reach for the opportunities, the practical, technical education so desired in Organisation Man's day is necessary, but far from sufficient for us.

TACT

Japan, outwardly such an awesome display of technical logic and discipline, cherishes the most subtle appreciation of the individual, each in his own personal space. Perhaps encouraged by the need to defer in an over-crowded archipelago; perhaps conditioned by Confucian concerns for human relationships, the ceremonial behaviour of the Japanese reveals a pervasive recognition that the values of others count. An eminent man like Koji Yamazaki, Japan's Governor of the International Monetary Fund, entertains at home with an unassuming delicacy that is a civilising force in itself.

We see in the *Nōh* plays fine distinctions, all the more discriminating for the formal structure against which they are worked out. The tea ceremony, far from an exclusively feminine prettiness, has developed over 500 hundred years a fine tact for the moment and the participants.[9] The Japanese tea-master, *chajin*, chooses his Ming porcelain with the most delicate propriety to complement the season, the event, or the visitor. A decoration of flowering plum twigs for late winter; travellers approaching a town gate with welcoming flags; the riverside scholar or the tiger to flatter merchant or samurai. The minutely frayed edge of unprotected glaze – *mushi-kui*, insect-nibbled – for the rustic hint. The *chajin* flourishes today; Japan, that hyper-efficient economic power, works because its people relate to each other in mutual respect, as Karel van Wolferen illustrates in *The Enigma of Japanese Power*.[10] He shows, for example, how informal and personal, and therefore perhaps effective, are the relationships among the Ministry of Finance, the Ministry of International Trade and Industry, and the great conglomerates; observations confirmed by westerners like Christopher Ryder, long the Swire Group's man in Tokyo, while he may differ from van Wolferen's more extreme observations. The humane arts seem crucial to personal and corporate success in the world's most impressive economy; business entertaining forms around 15 per cent of GNP. Five people can enjoy tea in a *chajin*'s pavilion for $10,000, two-thirds of that sum for a few impeccably presented morsels from rare and perfect fish or lobster. For most though, it's executive golf, which is no doubt capable of similar refinements.

ADMIRE OR EMULATE?

Correlli Barnett suggests that Leonardo da Vinci should be our inspiration. Perhaps that is right, but rather sad that so many of his ideas were neither practical nor implemented; rather discouraging that he was so obviously a loner. Perhaps, rather, we should emulate those who are able to combine a deep understanding of their fellow men with exemplary professional skill. I would settle for the Emperor Augustus, who not only built an empire out of chaos, but enjoyed it in peace, along with almost all its citizens. Patron of Horace, Virgil, and Vitruvius, he left the world a fruitful legacy. Horace to remind a war-ravaged people of the ethics of good citizens; Virgil to fill them with pride in their nation and its agriculture; then a great handbook of technology. Vitruvius had it all there; how to build a villa or a temple; specifications for the water engineer, the siege specialist, and the clock maker.

Right through the history of the world we can find extraordinary men and women who have lifted the aspirations and the achievement of whole peoples. There they are, different professions and different skills, but one common quality: the ability to understand the springs of human behaviour, and the power to inspire enthusiasm. Education for capability: competence in creating wealth, breadth to comprehend the views of others, and the sympathy to do so. Those surely are the qualities for success in our era. A liberal education concerned with the substance rather than textual scholasticism; an opening of the mind to the concepts and philosophy of science; and the ability to work with others fruitfully towards common goals. Educate citizens, and then develop leaders.

Educating for life

How, then, should young people be formed so that they can enjoy the new era and prosper in it? Broadly, is the answer surely. In the United States, the New Trier High Schools and Princeton have been doing it for years. In Britain, the national curriculum is bringing some welcome developments. Science, technology, mathematics, and English for everyone from five years old to sixteen must be good news, helping to bridge that gap in comprehension between those with a numerate and technical cast of mind and the rest. Testing what a child has understood by the ages of seven, eleven, fourteen and sixteen, expecting teachers to bring everyone up to a minimum level in each attainment target in each core subject, should prevent that sense of being left hopelessly behind that breeds despair.

So some of what Herbert Spencer was calling for all those years ago is coming through now. But how to make sure that the best of the humane themes are preserved too? A structure for scholarship is certainly needed, with its rigour, to cultivate the sharp edge in everyone's mind and form a base for some to build on later. Crucial, though, to draw out the aspects of human behaviour and ideas, as the best teachers can do rather well now, playing down all those excruciating dry rules and facts that kill interest in all but the passionately committed. Parsing an English passage and construing Caesar is all fortunately much less dominant than it was forty years ago; fortunate, because, under scholasticism, one may sacrifice the message for the medium; learn the rules of grammar, but loathe the literature. Pope hits at Richard Bentley in the *Dunciad*:[11]

> Thy mighty Scholiast, whose unwearied pains
> Made Horace dull, and humbled Milton's strains.

Endlessly grinding through passages of the Gallic wars, missing the thrill of the story for the ablative of quality, killed all pleasure in Latin for me for thirty years.

Surely then, a firm basic competence in science, technology and mathematics, and an affectionate familiarity with the liberal arts, must be the sound intellectual background for citizens in the society we can expect. And what of specialism? Surely everyone needs at least one subject grasped and mastered? Yes, but not to the exclusion of those other essentials, sacrificed so easily when the age of Organisation Man worshipped specialisation alone. Speaking in 1989, Sir Rolf Dahrendorf had no doubt that universities were necessary in distinction to technical colleges, educating rather than training for a vocation, but he was not sure whether Britain needed forty-seven. Should there be more, taking ground from the polytechnics, fewer, or just two? Mind you, he was speaking at an Oxbridge occasion, so maybe he was teasing the audience. In the United States, the Ivy League universities are not seen as irrelevant elites in the Midwest or Texas. Ohio State and Austin are cradles of classical learning; in Canada, Victoria College, Toronto is the world centre for lovers of Coleridge and of Erasmus.

I fear the longer-term effect of training that is too closely matched to a particular vocation; we have seen how much every walk of life has changed in the past few years, making old skills obsolete. Would young people not have safer prospects if they learned how to learn, whatever form of tertiary education they followed? The specific scientific facts I acquired at Cambridge have rarely been particularly relevant to any job that came my way, but that polymath framework has been extraordinarily helpful in getting usefully familiar with technologies as diverse as silicon integrated circuits, crystals for lasers, digital telecoms, artificial intelligence, ice cream, tobacco, and coffee! Training for a butterfly mind, some might say, but not so uncommon to future careers as in the past. Whatever the nature of that early education, though, the need to keep on learning is there for everyone. Any teacher who blunts that desire, in pursuit of some narrow body of facts firmly fixed, has damaged a vital asset.

I fear too neglect of the humanities. A Renaissance copy of Quintilian carries the message: "his studiis te applica, unde non iniuria maiores nostri omnem et humanitatis, et civilium rationum laudem petebant" ("Apply yourself then to these studies, whence not unjustly our ancestors sought the praise of humanity and of civilised judgement"). Though no doubt not sufficient for all the demands of our technical age, can we prosper without those insights?

NOTES

1 Correlli Barnett, *The Audit of War* (Papermac, London, 1987), p. 216.

2 Jonathan Swift, *An Account of a Battel between the Ancient and Modern Books in St James's Library* (Nutt, London, 1704), p. 251.

3 In Q. Horatius Flaccus, ed. Richard Bentley (Cambridge, 1711), p. 145 (*Notae et Emendationes*).

4 Augustine of Hippo, *Opuscula, Confessionum: Liber XI*, ed. Ascenius (Petit, Paris, 1513), p. 153.

5 Hugh Blair, *Lectures on Rhetoric and Belles Lettres* (Strahan, Cadell, Creech; London and Edinburgh, 1783).

6 Edward Corbett, *Classical Rhetoric for the Modern Student* (Oxford University Press, New York, 1971).

7 Erasmus, *The Praise of Folly*, tr. H. H. Hudson (Princeton University Press, New Jersey, 1974), pp. 131–42.

8 M. Tullius Cicero, *Ad M. Brutum, Orator*, ed. Schrevelius (Hackius, Leiden, 1661), p. 168.
9 Colin Sheaf and Michael Hughes, *The Peony Pavilion Collection* (Christie, Manson and Woods, London, 1989).
10 Karel van Wolferen, *The Enigma of Japanese Power* (Macmillan, London, 1989).
11 Alexander Pope, *Works*, vol. IV, ed. W. Roscoe (Rivington et al., London, 1824), p. 293.

13

RENAISSANCE

RIDING THE WHIRLWIND

JOSEPH Addison, in *The Campaign*, gave us a powerful metaphor for the individual triumphing over turbulence, in John Churchill, Duke of Marlborough, commanding at the battle of Blenheim:

'Twas then great Marlborough's mighty soul was proved,
That, in the shock of charging hosts unmoved,
Amidst confusion, horror, and despair,
Examined all the dreadful scenes of war:
In peaceful thought the field of death surveyed,
To fainting squadrons sent the timely aid,
Inspired repulsed battalions to engage,
And taught the doubtful battle where to rage.

In the fast-changing scenes of our own lives, physically peaceful but buffeted by the force of new technology unhampered by barriers to trade, that image should inspire. The Renaissance Man we need to follow is not an introverted genius like Leonardo, conceiving visions in a private world. Our example needs to be the fully formed, effective human being, self-possessed in conflict, reading the battle, perceiving with sympathy the reaction of others to the stress and opportunities of the times, each in the context of their own personal values. Ours is an age for leaders; now initiative passes to the individual.

In our era, Field Marshal Montgomery gives competence due weight:[1]

When all is said and done, the true leader must be able to dominate, and finally to master, the events which surround him; once he lets events get the better of him, those under him will lose confidence in him, and he will cease to be of value as a leader.

But he recognises the human dimension:[2]

The leader must also have a genuine interest in, and a real knowledge of humanity – which will always be the raw material of his trade. He must understand that bottled up in men are great emotional forces and these must have an outlet in a way which is positive and constructive, and which will warm their hearts and excite their imagination. If this can be done, and the forces can be harnessed and directed towards a common purpose, the greatest achievements become possible.

And that interest in the other person is not just for your own team and for the customer; your opponent too, is worthy of study. Montgomery had in his headquarters a picture of his great adversary Rommel, where it could remind him that the competitor has his options too; judging which he may choose is likely to be more accurate if his thought process can be imagined. A football coach tries to do that; good businessmen also. Slim found out all he could about General Kawabe, commanding Japanese forces in Burma, and pinned his photograph to the wall. He concluded: "a bold tactical planner of offensive movements, completely confident in the superiority of his troops, and prepared to use his last reserves rather than abandon a plan".[3] Sun Tzu summed it up more than 2,000 years ago: "Know the enemy and know yourself; in a hundred battles you will never be in peril."[4] Mao Tse-tung repeated the phrase. Now Komatsu have a man in Peoria, Illinois, watching Caterpillar; IBM have assigned a watcher to BT for years!

THE GOOD CITIZEN

So, narrow formation of the individual is no precept for success, now that the old certainties of the post-war world have been swept away. Thirty years ago, perhaps, in the functional structures of the day, as economies emerging from war called insatiably for skills in short supply. Then it did seem that honing the specialism was the way to be indispensable; although even that goal seemed dubious when, once reached, it proved to be a gilded cage.

Today, every sort of organisation needs men and women to match the new renaissance. Educated to understand the whole process of wealth creation; sympathetic, to judge soundly what others value; competent, to deliver that value economically; creative, resilient, inspiring their fellow men and women. Impossible? Only for the rare natural genius? Not so, I believe, if we are able to bridge the two cultures – the Arts and the Sciences – that have been separated for so long in the triumph of specialisation. That does not mean, as many contend, merely that the boundary should be shifted – more scientists or engineers, or information technologists or biochemists. Rather that everyone should be able to grasp the principles of science and its way of approaching the world; that everyone should be able to find that key to understanding men, where it lies in the liberal arts, long hidden so deftly by scholasticism. We need our particular excellences, but we need to be full human beings too.

AND THE STATE

For some in government to disclaim responsibility for curing these schisms, asserting that this is all an affair for the individual, is to follow a dangerous half-truth. Each one of us has, no doubt, his own responsibility to develop as a rounded citizen, but can there be a more fruitful task for government? Once the essential frameworks for defence and law have been set up, developing well-balanced people throughout a society surely brings the richest harvest in both economic and political fruits.

In Britain, for example, the marked disparity between creativity in science and using those ideas commercially hints at deep divisions in our society, stemming from our earliest ideas. The disdain of professionals for the merely commercial; of the public servant for the perceived petty dishonesties of the trader; of the businessman for the bureaucrat; scientists caricatured as boffins – characteristics of a society in which exclusivity has been a valued goal. Unless all those minds can be opened from the start, and right through education, only the naturally limber will be able to move freely among the attitudes and inclinations jostling in a richly varied and changing world. The damage may have been kindly meant: that conciliating permission to specialise early; the licence to drop a subject that is difficult or uncongenial; pot hunting, glorying in the exceptional while ignoring the silent child who finds it hard to keep up; these are the sins of pedagogues that have fostered the incomprehensions that plague us.

Is the scope, then, of the British national curriculum sound? Science, mathematics, and English look fine for the core, but how should the humanities fare? Can it be right to close the classical world to most of the new generation? And what if history is squeezed? Should the nasty tyrannies in the tabloids be the staple diet, or could, perhaps, some nodding acquaintance with extraordinary human beings of previous centuries start an interest in their diversity? How better to hook in some sense of social obligation than by relating the abuse of personal interest or its denial in the past – with the consequences there to be seen. And in the most direct commercial sense, some awareness of European, American and Asian history is surely essential to future citizens of the global society?

Japan's broad school curriculum and widespread further education must surely lie behind its success in getting things to work, because people work together. The insistence that outstanding young students divert their talents from personal exhibition to group support, "The nail that sticks up gets hammered down", may look odd to western societies with our admiration for the exceptional, but which philosophy is more likely to foster a culture amenable to mutual understanding? Perhaps one might sardonically observe that our structured, specialised society has been more noted – as Japan's MITI reports – for spectacular leaps in the creation of knowledge. But who gathers the harvest? Is the reaper less worthy than the sower? He certainly gets richer!

In the United States, where conditions allow, young people do start out on the humane path. The best of the nation's High Schools see that all their students begin college careers with English, mathematics, science, history, and a foreign language in their mental equipment. The Ivy League see that the early years of college keep minds open across the field of humane knowledge. A sound beginning, but sadly not proof against the pressure later to conform to one special interest or another. Some force pushes so many into segregation; the rules of each separate game seem to form blinkered protagonists. The lawyers pursuing selfish advantage to the very limits of the letter; the utility managers playing the formulae for rate setting with scant concern for sensible economics; the technical men scornful of lay uncertainties; bankers rigging the market.

So it is not enough just to stock minds with broad knowledge; we all need people who can retain a generous understanding under pressure, and who wish to go on learning. Those are the characteristics that education should stimulate, rather than exclusively practical skills, soon to be outdated, or liberal knowledge unrelated to life – or to principle. Strength of character that can keep good sense and common humanity – even when the narrow constraints persist; the Victorians had something in their value system worth rediscovery.

If government, then, must be concerned in shaping the young, it inevitably shapes much more too. Corporatism created Organisation Man, and the most powerful corporation of all is government. Resoundingly true in continental Europe, wherever Napoleon's influence remains; true too in the United States, although separation of powers brings variety and remarkable visibility to the process. Separation of powers legislative, legal, and executive; between federal and state; between Cabinet functions, gives individuality plenty of scope to flourish! But though not monolithic, government in the United States is certainly pervasive, but disintegrated. Where else in the world can one find the equal to the Washington lobbyist? Robert Horton, fresh from the experience of running Sohio, testifies to the patronage of particular politicians in defining – or changing – the rules affecting the success of business. In telecommunications, MCI no doubt had a major engineering and marketing task in challenging Bell, but surely owed its commercial success to skill in playing the Washington game: easy terms for interconnection and damages for delay. What a use for human talent! Machiavelli would have felt at home.

If every action and inaction of government bears on how people act, then surely some form of national strategy, some understood frame in which free citizens can work, needs to be fashioned through the political process? Right through this book has run the theme that structure is necessary to fruitful creation, but that framework must be right for the age and for the nature of the people. It helps to understand what will be valued, not just what is forbidden; good managers encourage allies to converge their efforts, so why not government? Is creating an explicit national strategy too difficult, or too embarrassing? It certainly need not mean anything so specific as picking winners; more the statement of national aspiration that Japan's MITI has promoted so successfully.

THE CHANGING ESTABLISHMENT

There is more to changing style than lies within the sphere of government, however active. Every nation has its establishment, and each by its nature is resistant to change. There they are, all sorts of self-perpetuating bodies, fashioned when special skills were prized in isolation, consolidating values and perceptions. A crucial group among them, the professional institutes face radical changes. Limited by their charters to a scope that carefully skirts the territory of others, with strongly entrenched schemes of expertise and of qualification, governed by their members, those proud oligarchies may find it hard to adapt to the new realities.

Do they need to change? After all, some of the most successful banks were those that resisted the received wisdom of the financial supermarket, concentrating on doing well what they knew. I believe they must, because their members must. Few professionals can dodge the convergence of disciplines, as the functional baronies are broken down and decisions made fast, near to the market place. So for most, the future holds an unnerving step into unfamiliar territory. Brought up to the security of an accustomed set of experiences and pro-fessional rules, knowing they had done their duty beyond reproach – whatever the results, they will need help when those parameters do not meet the case. Where are they to get it from? Institutes proud of the distinctions that separate must seek the processes that can link them to their fellows. Why? Because their members need broader support.

Take, for example, the engineer who sets up a new business; certainly an urgent need there for financial advice and guidance in employment law. Quite paralysing at first to hire staff at your own expense, uncertain about redundancy pay or pregnancy leave! Where does the advice come from? Octagon, the venture capital firm, runs a club for its start-ups, where over 100 business tyros can exchange experiences. At Aston and at Cambridge, science parks offer incubators for new businesses, laying on specialist support from a central panel – but what of the rest? Surely we must see professional institutions linking to give their members a broad service to meet their broad needs, encouraging them to add other skills to the first – and of all those necessary new capabilities, none is more universal than the art of general management, the science of co-ordinating to achieve. New technology can help, here as in so many other ways, to mitigate the difficulties it gives rise to. Terminals can reach to databases across the telecom network, and clever software can take the complexity out of unfamiliar protocols; gateway systems can open up a dozen different sources of fact or advice to one familiar first data call. But those systems need to be devised, not, as in the past, for the expert checking in comfortable territory, but for novices tentatively probing beyond the bounds of their routine. Who are to design those systems? Can the professional establishment act in unusual co-operation?

AND THE EMPLOYER

And what of the employers? How strange that some fear to broaden the competence of their people – or at least to allow that to be signalled in a recognised qualification – lest they move on! A fallacy in logic surely, to infer that new MBAs will change their employer, because job changers often take that qualification as a springboard to a new career. Thus, even though almost every organisation needs more people capable of moving confidently into fresh fields, some still hold back from the recognised courses that can bring those insights. Why, it is the mentality of the seraglio and the chastity belt lingering from the feudal age, or the attitude of a Russian serf-master of the nineteenth century! So that needs to change, or perhaps the individual should just seize for himself what he will surely need.

Fortunately, though, the enlightened employers are there to show that investing in people creates wealth, even though a few may stray. Those vigorous wealth creators in the free cities of Germany 500 years ago moved around Europe, to the benefit of that empire, bringing prosperity to their native cities as they went. Of course, sometimes a fool kicked over the system, like that bishop who sacked Mainz, and spread the first printers all over Europe, to the good fortune of Italy, where fruitful entrepreneurs were always welcome. Even some of the employers who do value trained managers are sufficiently trapped in the old inward attitudes to prefer internal courses, like the in-company MBA's. Hard to understand really, when so few businesses can expect a future much like the past. Consortium courses seem much more to the point, like the MBA set up in Britain by BP, Coopers and Lybrand, National Westminster Bank, and the Metropolitan Police in 1989.

WHICH PATTERN?

As we broach the new era, in which more of the world's people than ever before are capable of being players in a world economy, which of the many patterns will work best? Where in the spectrum from Prince Kropotkin's anarchy to Stalin's state tyranny, does the fruitful social and economic structure lie? How can the energy of the individual be set loose, and yet society prosper?

We see Japan succeeding mightily in commerce, where individuality is submerged in the group and decisions made in concert, or at least after a thoroughness of consultation unusual in the West. But will its formula succeed when others seize the initiative and force the pace? Two lines from Ogden Nash, in another context:[5]

> You look divine as you advance,
> Have you seen yourself retreating?

Is the Japanese passion for consensus and the suppression of personal initiative, perhaps suitable for the deliberate strategy in assault, possible when the competitor is peaceful, complacent, or sluggish in response? Forty-five years ago Japan seemed irresistible in South East Asia and the Pacific, until the tide of war turned against it. Then, in the hustle of retreat, wrong-footed and suicidal under pressure, as Bougainville and the bypassing strategy of Admiral Nimitz and General MacArthur revealed in the Pacific. Field Marshal Slim, after retreat and then victory in Burma, observed[6] "I had not realised how the Japanese, formidable as long as they are allowed to follow undisturbed their daring projects, are thrown into confusion by the unexpected." So, while the power of concerted effort is there to admire, judicious emulation seems wise if you cannot dominate; cherish the individual – you may need his verve! Those Japanese destroyer commanders at the battle of Tassafaronga off Guadalcanal,[7] showed what could be done against superior forces when initiative was given free play; perhaps that was the Nelson spirit at work!

The United States admires the egregious, valuing the exceptional, still fostering that pursuit of specialist excellence noted by W. H. Whyte, whatever admirable breadth there may be in its best schools and colleges. The constraints that have proved necessary to protect society from the extremes of self-interest, create a jungle of quasi-legal rules, a pasture for the lawyers, and unresisted encouragement to test the letter rather than follow the spirit of the law. Experts – in space, nuclear energy, utilities, in defence and more – singlemindedly pursue their own solutions through the lobbies, intent on outwitting those outside their own coteries. Still impressively successful in commerce; admired everywhere as an archetype of freedom, is that style to be followed blindly? Perhaps only a very rich economy could afford the energy lost in so much friction!

Europe, the continent still influenced in so many ways by Napoleon, with his concept, drawn from Louis XIV and modified by the Revolution, of society dominated by the State, with men protected by rights rather than mutual obligations, has its rich variety of structures, soon to come under the test of open competition in an integrated market. Whose pattern will inspire the others? West Germany preserves the cartel and an ordered economy, and yet is triumphantly successful in international trade. Are those controls going to survive the new turbulence at home? Sweden has a welfare state as pervasive as any and heavy taxes on higher incomes, but flourishes in advanced technology around the world. France trains an exceptional elite, permeates the decision making of Europe, but what of the middle ground between the renowned business sense of the *petite bourgeoisie* and the huge corporation? Have they got the conditions for an enterprise culture? Britain has exposed its economy to unbridled international competition, and is developing its own fresh styles of leadership and in personal relationships, but still cannot cause national inventiveness to bear its harvest at home; still cannot harness the spirit of individuals in cohesive strategy; is still anorexic in the urge to cut costs, rather than add muscle and value.

Russia and its satellites are tentatively forming new societies, after their disastrous experiments with utopianism. But, while Czecho-slovakia may call on a recent past in which the individual flourished in commerce and scholarship, and remind itself of a Bohemia that was the artistic glory of the Holy Roman Empire, what of Russia? Are Russians, after centuries of unrelieved feudal autocracy, capable of initiative? The other communist colossus has a richer loam to cultivate. Will the venerable Chinese mercantile qualities be allowed to blossom on the mainland, as they have done so impressively in Singapore, Hong Kong, and Taiwan? Around the globe, com-munities from Gambia to Canton are flexing trading capabilities that have long been suppressed or constrained; perhaps as freedom comes, they will flower like the desert after rain.

FOR A TURBULENT FUTURE

All those societies have achieved their successes and their failures in a world that is vanishing; within a structure of international relationships formed for a world weary of the chaos of war. What will work best in the new turbulence? In nations and in the organ-isation, the same paradox must be resolved: set the people free to unleash their individual energy, and yet harness them to achieve corporate goals. As we move from ordered to turbulent conditions, for most the balance will shift towards freedom, accepting untidiness in untidy circumstances; but indiscipline brings its dangers. Caesar at the Sambre showed how necessary cohesion could be in defence; the Japanese businessman that it works in attack too.

So what to do? One principle seems safe: focus minds on the achievement rather than the process, the result rather than the method. If that is combined with a division of the corporate goal into modules, each with its interface to the whole defined, but the rest left free for initiative, then at least the burden of one level of authority is lessened, without diminishing co-ordination where it matters, and eyes will be turned outwards to the opportunity. If that architecture is matched with the vector of an explicit strategy, one can hope for something more: initiative outside the module, helpful to the wider objective. Perhaps that strategy could go some way to unleashing Montgomery's great emotional forces!

There cannot be one answer, surely. In the West, 3,000 years of recorded social relationships have seen the gamut, from rigid tyranny of persons and ideas to episodes of extraordinary creativity; sympathy and human happiness have flourished for a while, until one single-issue fanatic or another has broken through the limits within which freedom must always be regulated. Each society has its own history.

Within that broad spectrum, latent values allow different options, depending on the condition of our particular collective memory. But in our new age of turbulence and global opportunity, one theme seems clear: the new era needs the individual, as a free spirit, not Burckhardt's feudal man, "Conscious of himself only as a member of a race, people, party, family, or corporation."[8] Few will spend a career with one employer; even those that do will find that employer quite different after thirty years, or after ten. A narrow capability may be safe for a few, but not for most; learning is lifelong. The possibilities for everyone capable of rational thought and human sympathy are quite extraordinary, exceeding those few miraculous periods in the past when the human spirit triumphed over the chains of introversion and bureaucracy. That delicate awareness of the other person in his living space found in the tea ceremony, combined with the purposeful conciliations of MITI, is likely to work more fruitfully than Vanderbilt's, "The Public be damned". But turbulence is rich in energy; so it must be sympathy with vigour, working with the grain of forces in play, but creative in opportunity – riding the whirlwind and directing the storm.

NOTES

1 Field Marshal B. L. Montgomery, *The Path to Leadership* (Putnam, New York, 1961), p. 12.
2 Ibid.
3 Field Marshal W. J. Slim, *Defeat into Victory* (Papermac, London, 1986), p. 221.
4 Sun Tzu, *The Art of War*, tr. Samuel Griffith (Oxford University Press, Oxford, 1963), p. 84.
5 Ogden Nash, "What's the Use", in *Verses 1929* (Little Brown and Co., 1959), p. 103.
6 Slim, *Defeat into Victory*, p. 121.
7 E. B. Potter, *Bull Halsey*, (Naval Institute Press, Annapolis, 1988), p. 187–189.
8 Jacob Burckhardt, *The Civilization of the Renaissance in Italy*, tr. S. G. C. Middlemore (Phaedon, Vienna, n.d.), p. 70.

INDEX